Power Maths

Year 2 Textb

Series Editor: Tony Staneff

Sparks

Sparks is helpful.

He likes to help if you get stuck.

curious

Ash

brave

Astrid

determined

Dexter

flexible

Flo

 **Pearson**

Contents

This shows us what page to turn to.

Are you ready for the next part of our maths journey?

How to use this book

Do you remember how to use Power Maths?

These pages help us get ready for a new unit.

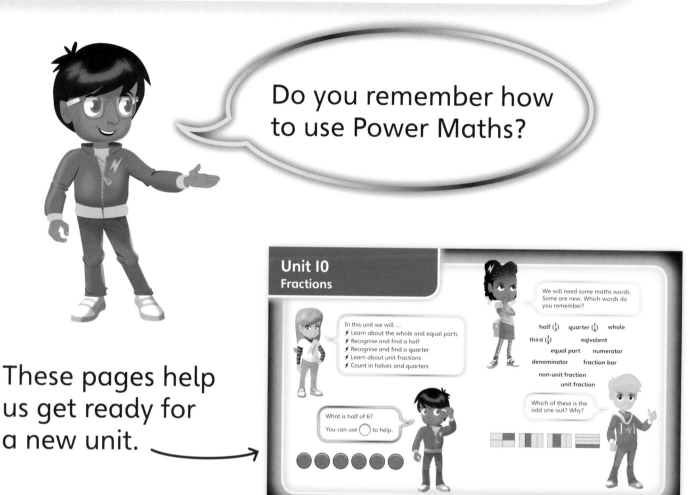

Discover

Lessons start with Discover.

Have fun exploring new maths problems.

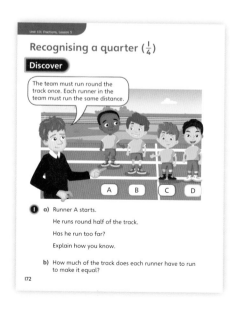

Share

Next, we share what we found out.

Did we all solve the problems the same way?

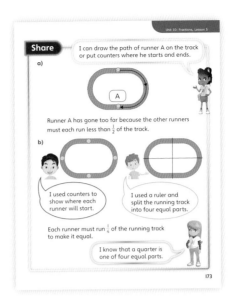

Think together

Then we have a go at some more problems together.

We will try a challenge too!

This tells you which page to go to in your Practice Book.

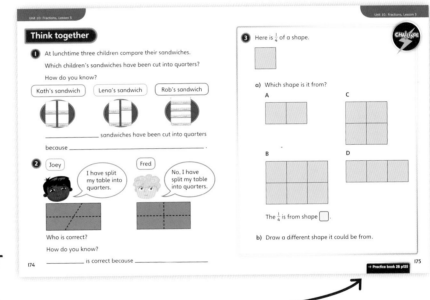

At the end of a unit we will show how much we can do!

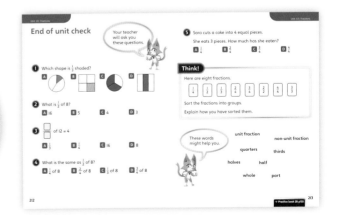

Unit 6
Multiplication and division ②

In this unit we will ...
- ⚡ Divide by 2
- ⚡ Learn about odd and even numbers
- ⚡ Divide by 5 and 10
- ⚡ Divide by grouping and by sharing
- ⚡ Use related multiplication facts to solve division problems

You have used equal sharing before. How would you share 6 🍓 between 2 people?

We will need some maths words. Have you used some of these words before?

divide (÷)   **division**

share   **group**

odd   **even**   **times-table**

Do you remember how to use grouping? How many groups of 2 ◯ are there in 8 ◯ ?

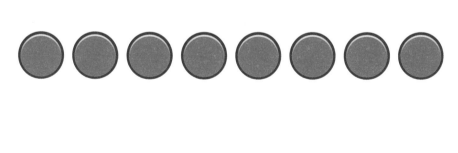

Making equal groups

Discover

1 **a)** 12 children want to dance in groups of 4.

How many groups are there?

b) The 12 children now dance in groups of 3.

How many groups are there now?

There will be 3 3 groups.

Share

a)

I can see that each round of sharing must give everyone exactly the same until all the are shared.

I can give the apples away until I have none left. I can use a division sentence to represent this.

There are 6 apples.

They are shared between 3 friends.

We can write this as $6 \div 3 = 2$

Each friend gets 2 🍎 .

b) There are 9 pears.

They are shared between 3 friends.

$9 \div 3 = 3$

Each friend gets 3 🍐 .

Think together

1. There are 6  in a bowl to share between 2 children.

   Use drawings to show this and write the division sentence.

I will use counters to represent the ⬤.

There are ▢ oranges.

We share them between ▢ people.

Each person gets ▢ each.

So 6 ÷ ▢ = ▢ .

2. There are 10 🍓 in a bowl to share between 5 children.

   Use counters to help you. Use drawings to show this and write the division sentence.

▢ ÷ ▢ = ▢

14

3

8 ◯ are shared between 2 friends.

Roxy writes a number sentence to show this.

8 ÷ 2 = 4

What does the 8 represent?

What does the 2 represent?

What does the 4 represent?

Do the same with another number sentence.

I wonder what the difference is between sharing and grouping.

15

Dividing by 2

Discover

I **a)** 8 players practise in pairs.

How many groups of 2 are there?

$8 \div 2 = \boxed{}$

b)

> I worked it out using $4 \times 2 = 8$ from the 2 times-table.

Explain how Flo used that number fact to solve the problem.

Share

a)

I used a drawing to help me.

I used the 2 times-table to help me.

8 players make 4 pairs.

Keep subtracting 2 from 8. You can subtract it 4 times.

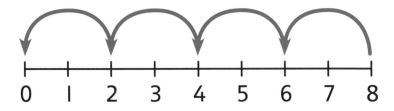

$8 \div 2 = 4$

There are 4 groups of 2.

b) There are 8 players. There are 2 players in each group.

The drawing reminds me that 4 groups of 2 is 8. So $8 \div 2 = 4$.

$1 \times 2 = 2$
$2 \times 2 = 4$
$3 \times 2 = 6$
$4 \times 2 = 8$
$5 \times 2 = 10$
$6 \times 2 = 12$
$7 \times 2 = 14$
$8 \times 2 = 16$
$9 \times 2 = 18$

17

Think together

1 2 more players want to join in.

How many groups of 2 can be made now?

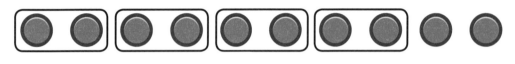

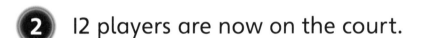

$5 \times 2 = 10$

So $10 \div 2 = \boxed{}$.

$1 \times 2 = 2$
$2 \times 2 = 4$
$3 \times 2 = 6$
$4 \times 2 = 8$
$5 \times 2 = 10$
$6 \times 2 = 12$
$7 \times 2 = 14$
$8 \times 2 = 16$
$9 \times 2 = 18$

2 12 players are now on the court.

How many groups of 2 can these players make?

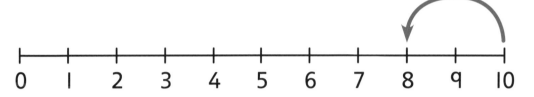

$\boxed{} \times 2 = \boxed{}$ so $12 \div 2 = \boxed{}$.

What if there were 14 players, 16 players or 18 players?

$1 \times 2 = 2$
$2 \times 2 = 4$
$3 \times 2 = 6$
$4 \times 2 = 8$
$5 \times 2 = 10$
$6 \times 2 = 12$
$7 \times 2 = 14$
$8 \times 2 = 16$
$9 \times 2 = 18$

18

3 Every 2 players can be paired up for practising tennis. On a 100 square, colour the numbers that can be divided by 2 or use counters to mark them.

Did you find a pattern?

1	2	3	4	5	6	7	8	9	10
11	12	13	14	15	16	17	18	19	20
21	22	23	24	25	26	27	28	29	30
31	32	33	34	35	36	37	38	39	40
41	42	43	44	45	46	47	48	49	50
51	52	53	54	55	56	57	58	59	60
61	62	63	64	65	66	67	68	69	70
71	72	73	74	75	76	77	78	79	80
81	82	83	84	85	86	87	88	89	90
91	92	93	94	95	96	97	98	99	100

What do you notice about which columns the numbers are in?

19

→ Practice book 2B p12

Odd and even numbers

Discover

1 **a)** Which socks can be sorted into pairs with none left over?

b) More socks are hung out to dry.

Can each row be sorted into pairs with none left over?

Write Yes or No for your answer.

8		
9		
10		
11		
12		

Share

a) Each pair of socks has 2 socks.

I circled each pair but there is 1 sock left over.

The plain socks can be sorted into pairs with none left over.

b)

I counted in 2s to see which socks could be paired up. 2, 4, 6, 8, 10...

8	![striped socks]	yes
9	![spotted socks]	no
10	![spotted socks]	yes
11	![checked socks]	no
12	![plain socks]	yes

2, 4, 6, 8, 10 and 12 are **even** numbers.
1, 3, 5, 7, 9 and 11 are **odd** numbers.

Think together

1 A shop buys 14 wheels.

A needs 2 wheels.

Can all the wheels be paired up?

Copy the diagram and complete the sentences.

14 wheels _____ be paired up.

14 is an _____ number.

can	cannot
odd	even

2 Can 15 wheels be paired up?

Copy the diagram and complete the sentences.

15 wheels _____ be paired up.

15 is an _____ number.

3 **a)** Is 17 an odd or even number?

b) Sort these numbers to show whether they are odd or even.

| 16 | 17 | 20 | 25 | 32 | 33 |

Odd	Even
9 11	10

CHALLENGE

I will group them into 2s.

I think I have found a quicker way.

→ Practice book 2B p15

Dividing by 5

Discover

1 **a)**

There are 20 ⬤.

Each flower needs 5 ⬤.

How many flowers can you make with 20 ⬤?

b)

> I worked it out using 4 × 5 = 20 from the 5 times-table.

Explain how Flo used that number fact to solve the problem and complete the number sentence.

20 ÷ 5 = ☐

Share

I used a drawing to help me.

a)

I used the 5 times-table to help me. $4 \times 5 = 20$.

Keep subtracting 5 from 20. You can subtract 4 times.

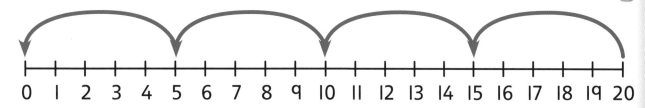

You can make 4 flowers with 20 🌢.

b)

There are 20 🌢. Every 5 🌢 is one group.

The drawing reminds me that 4 groups of 5 is 20, $4 \times 5 = 20$.

So $20 \div 5 = 4$.

$1 \times 5 = 5$
$2 \times 5 = 10$
$3 \times 5 = 15$
$4 \times 5 = 20$
$5 \times 5 = 25$
$6 \times 5 = 30$
$7 \times 5 = 35$
$8 \times 5 = 40$
$9 \times 5 = 45$

Think together

I wonder if I could use the 5 times-table to help.

1   Every 5 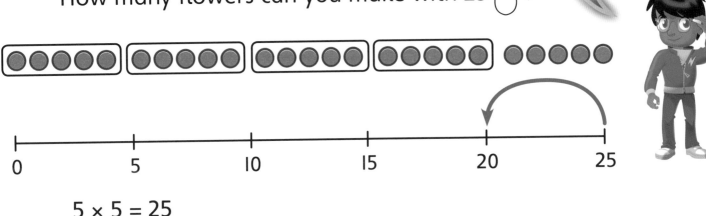 make one flower.

How many flowers can you make with 25 ◇ ?

$5 \times 5 = 25$

So $25 \div 5 = \boxed{}$.

2   How many flowers can you make with 30 ◇ ?

What if there were 35 ◇ or 40 ◇ ?

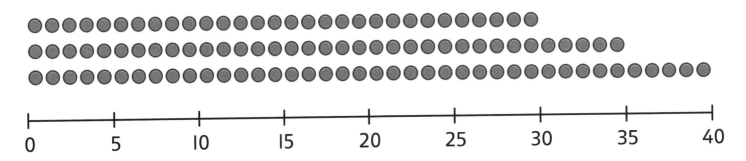

$6 \times 5 = \boxed{}$ so $30 \div 5 = \boxed{}$.

$\boxed{} \times 5 = 35$ so $35 \div 5 = \boxed{}$.

$\boxed{} \times \boxed{} = \boxed{}$ so $40 \div 5 = \boxed{}$.

3 Every 5  can make one flower.

On a 100 square, colour the numbers that can make flowers or use counters to mark them.

Did you find a pattern?

1	2	3	4	5	6	7	8	9	10
11	12	13	14	15	16	17	18	19	20
21	22	23	24	25	26	27	28	29	30
31	32	33	34	35	36	37	38	39	40
41	42	43	44	45	46	47	48	49	50
51	52	53	54	55	56	57	58	59	60
61	62	63	64	65	66	67	68	69	70
71	72	73	74	75	76	77	78	79	80
81	82	83	84	85	86	87	88	89	90
91	92	93	94	95	96	97	98	99	100

I saw a pattern going down.

27

→ Practice book 2B p18

Dividing by 10

Discover

Marta Sam Josh

1 a) There are 30 ✏.

How many packs of 10 ✏ are there?

b)

> I worked it out using 3 × 10 = 30 from the 10 times-table.

Explain how Flo used that number fact to solve the problem and complete the number sentence.

30 ÷ 10 = ☐

Share

I used a drawing to help me.

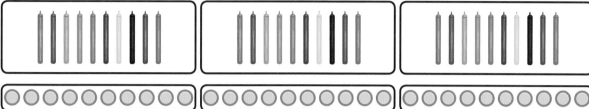

a)

$30 - 10 = 20$
$20 - 10 = 10$
$10 - 10 = 0$

Keep subtracting 10 from 30.
You can subtract it 3 times.

There are 3 packs of 10.

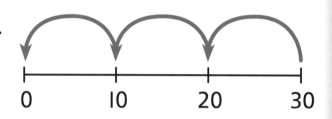

0   10   20   30

b) There are 30.

Every 10 is one group.

$1 \times 10 = 10$
$2 \times 10 = 20$
$3 \times 10 = 30$
$4 \times 10 = 40$
$5 \times 10 = 50$
$6 \times 10 = 60$
$7 \times 10 = 70$
$8 \times 10 = 80$

I used the 10 times-table to help me. $3 \times 10 = 30$.

The drawing reminds me that 3 groups of 10 is 30, $3 \times 10 = 30$.

So $30 \div 10 = 3$.

Think together

I wonder if I could use the 10 times-table to help me.

1 Every 10 ✏ make one pack.

How many packs can you make with 40 ✏ ?

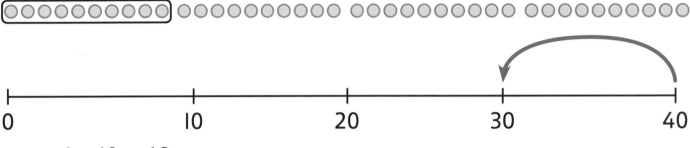

$4 \times 10 = 40$

So $40 \div 10 = \boxed{}$.

2 How many packs can you make with 50 ✏ ?

What if there were 60 ✏ or 80 ✏ ?

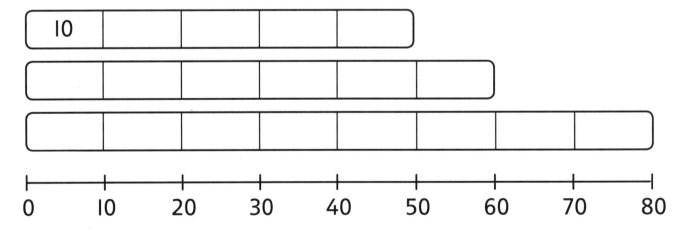

10				

$5 \times 10 = \boxed{}$ so $50 \div 10 = \boxed{}$.

$\boxed{} \times 10 = 60$ so $60 \div 10 = \boxed{}$.

$\boxed{} \times \boxed{} = \boxed{}$ so $80 \div 10 = \boxed{}$.

3 Every 10 ✏ make I pack.

On a 100 square, colour the numbers that can make packs or use counters to mark them.

Did you find a pattern?

1	2	3	4	5	6	7	8	9	10
11	12	13	14	15	16	17	18	19	20
21	22	23	24	25	26	27	28	29	30
31	32	33	34	35	36	37	38	39	40
41	42	43	44	45	46	47	48	49	50
51	52	53	54	55	56	57	58	59	60
61	62	63	64	65	66	67	68	69	70
71	72	73	74	75	76	77	78	79	80
81	82	83	84	85	86	87	88	89	90
91	92	93	94	95	96	97	98	99	100

What is the same about all the numbers you have highlighted? What is different about the numbers?

→ Practice book 2B p21

Bar modelling – grouping

Discover

1 **a)** 10 ⬚ can be carried on each tray.

How many trays are needed for 40 ⬚ ?

40 ÷ ☐ = ☐

b) 5 ⬚ can be carried on each tray.

How many trays are needed for 35 ⬚ ?

35 ÷ ☐ = ☐

Share

a)

The whole is 40. Each part is 10, but how many parts are there?

I drew a bar model to help me. Each time I added a bar with 10 until I got to 40.

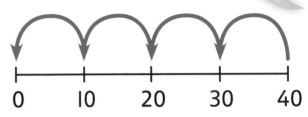

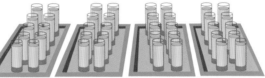

40

10	10	10	10

40 ÷ 10 = 4 so 4 trays are needed for 40 .

b)

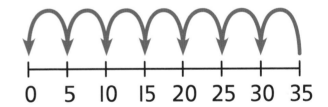

35

5	5	5	5	5	5	5

35 ÷ 5 = 7 so 7 trays are needed for 35 .

Think together

1. Another 60  are made.

How many more trays are needed?

```
                                                60
┌──────────────────────────────────────────────┴──────────────────┐
│ ┌──────────┬──────────┬ ─ ─ ─ ─ ─ ─ ─ ┐
│ │    10    │    10    ┆              ┆
│ └──────────┴──────────┴ ─ ─ ─ ─ ─ ─ ─ ┘
```

60 ÷ ☐ = ☐

There are ☐ more trays needed.

Remember that 10  fit on each tray.

2. Joe can only fit 3 bowls of crisps on each tray. There are 21 bowls of crisps.

How many trays will he need?

```
                              21
┌─────────────────────────────┴─────────────────────┐
│ ┌──────────┬ ─ ─ ─ ─ ─ ─ ┐
│ │    3     ┆            ┆
│ └──────────┴ ─ ─ ─ ─ ─ ─ ┘
```

☐ ÷ ☐ = ☐

34

3 Pari has 50 oranges.

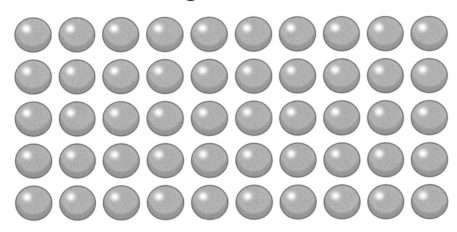

a) If she packs them into boxes of 10,
   how many boxes will she need?

   ⬜ ÷ ⬜ = ⬜

   She will need ⬜ boxes.

b) If she packs them into boxes of 5,
   how many boxes will she need?

   ⬜ ÷ ⬜ = ⬜

   She will need ⬜ boxes.

I can see a link
between $10 \times 5 = 50$
and the answers here.

35

→ Practice book 2B p24

Bar modelling – sharing

Discover

Share the treasures

1 **a)** 2 pirates share 12 ⬡ .

How many do they get each?

12 ÷ 2 = ☐

b) 3 pirates share 15 ◇ .

How many do they get each?

15 ÷ 3 = ☐

36

Share

a) There are 12 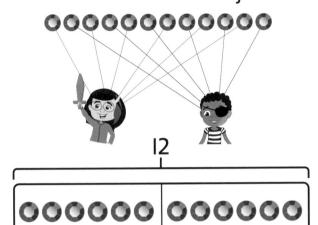 and 2 pirates.

We need to share the jewels out.

> There are 12 jewels and I shared them out one by one.

12

They get 6 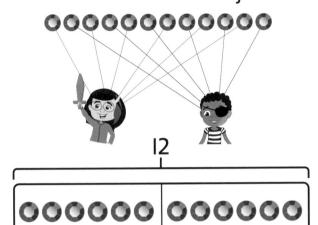 each.

$12 \div 2 = 6$

> I drew a bar model with 2 parts, because there are 2 pirates.

b) There are 15 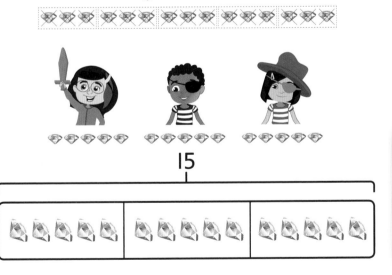 and 3 pirates.

15

> I will remove a group of 3 at a time and give one to each pirate. We are still sharing.

They get 5 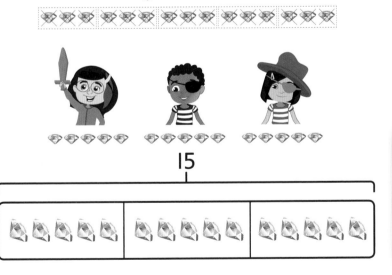 each.

$15 \div 3 = 5$

Think together

1 2 pirates share 18  . How many do they get each?

18

$$\boxed{} \div 2 = \boxed{}$$

2 4 pirates share 20 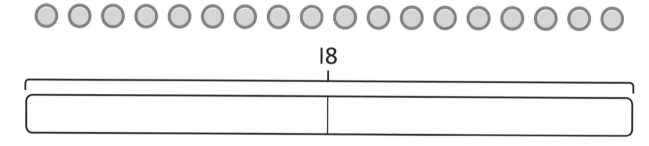 .

How many do they get each?

$$\boxed{} \div \boxed{} = \boxed{}$$

When I am sharing, I don't know how many each pirate will get until I have finished.

3 Tom wrote two division sentences.

$6 \div 3 = 2$

$8 \div 2 = 4$

Draw the matching bar models and sharing diagrams.

CHALLENGE

I can see which jewels they are sharing by looking at the picture.

Can you share out all the different jewels between the pirates?

Share the treasures

39

Solving word problems – division

Discover

1 **a)** The team have raised £80. They want to spend no more than £40 on .

Do they have enough to buy a 👕 for everyone?

Write the matching number sentence.

☐ ◯ ☐ ◯ ☐

b) What can they buy to spend all of the other £40?

How will you find out?

Write the matching number sentence.

☐ ◯ ☐ ◯ ☐

Share

I looked for information to help solve the problem.

I represented the problem in different ways.

a)

£40 is divided between the 5 members of the team.

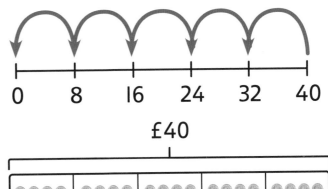

0   8   16   24   32   40

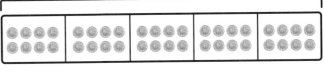

£40

A costs £8. Yes, they have enough to buy a for everyone.

$40 \div 5 = 8$.

b) £40 is divided between the 5 members of the team. Each team member has £8 to spend.

$40 \div 5 = 8$

£40

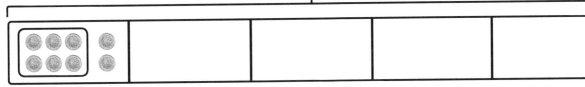

 + = £8.

Team members can each buy  and .

41

Think together

1. Each team member makes their own .

    Each  needs a 5 centimetre strip of fabric.

    They have 25 centimetres of fabric.

    How many  can they make?

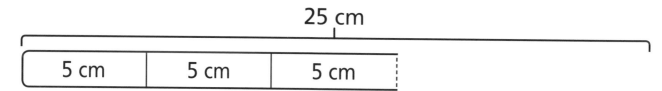

25 ÷ 5 = ☐

They can make ☐ .

2. The team raises another £50.

    Do they have enough to buy for everyone?

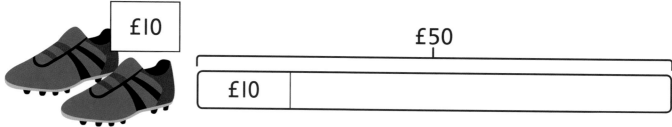

3 Solve one of these story problems.

a) I have £12 and plan to buy  for 3 friends.

How much can I spend on each friend?

b) I have £10 and plan to buy some

 which cost £2 each.

How many can I buy?

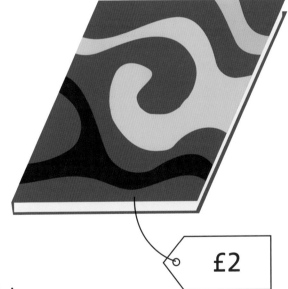

£2

Write your own story problem.

Swap it with a friend.

Can you solve their story problem?

43

→ Practice book 2B p30

End of unit check

Your teacher will ask you these questions.

1 Which division tells you how many groups?

A 20 ÷ 5 = 5   B 20 ÷ 5 = 4   C 20 ÷ 4 = 5   D 20 ÷ 4 = 4

2 James the farmer has 30 bales of hay.

He shares them between 5 fields.

Which diagram tells you how many bales for each field?

A
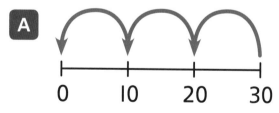

C
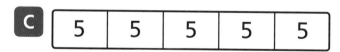

5	5	5	5	5

B
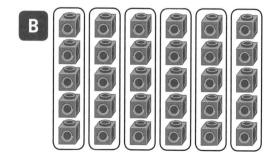

D
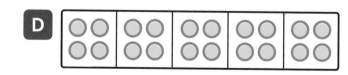

3 Which numbers complete the division?

$$25 \div \boxed{} = \boxed{}$$

A 1 and 5　　　**B** 5 and 5　　　**C** 5 and 10　　　**D** 25 and 5

4 Which division matches the multiplication?

$$8 \times 5 = 40$$

A $40 \div 5 = 8$　　**B** $8 \div 40 = 5$　　**C** $5 \times 8 = 40$　　**D** $5 \div 40 = 8$

Think!

Which numbers give an odd answer when you divide by 5? Colour them blue.

Which numbers give an odd answer when you divide by 10? Colour them yellow.

Can you continue the pattern for the whole square?

Explain the patterns.

1	2	3	4	5	6	7	8	9	10
11	12	13	14	15	16	17	18	19	20
21	22	23	24	25	26	27	28	29	30
31	32	33	34	35	36	37	38	39	40
41	42	43	44	45	46	47	48	49	50
51	52	53	54	55	56	57	58	59	60
61	62	63	64	65	66	67	68	69	70
71	72	73	74	75	76	77	78	79	80
81	82	83	84	85	86	87	88	89	90
91	92	93	94	95	96	97	98	99	100

These words might help you.

divide　　　odd　　　even

ten　　　digit　　　ones

→ Practice book 2B p33

Unit 7
Statistics

In this unit we will ...
- ⚡ Make tally charts
- ⚡ Use pictograms
- ⚡ Use block diagrams
- ⚡ Solve word problems

We will need to use tally charts. How many of each animal is there?

Here are some new maths words. Can you read them out loud?

tally chart   **pictogram**

key

We will also use pictograms. Who picked the most apples?

Name	Number
Tariq 🍎🍎🍎🍎🍎🍎🍎🍎🍎🍎
Amy 🍎🍎🍎🍎🍎🍎🍎

Making tally charts

Discover

1 a) Tariq and Amy are playing a game.

How many games did each child win?

b) Who won overall? Tariq or Amy? How do you know?

Share

Tariq	Amy
IIIIIIII IIIIIIII IIII	IIIIIIII IIIIIIII IIIIIIII III

a) Count each of Tariq's tally marks.

There are 18 for Tariq and 24 for Amy.

Count Amy's tally marks in groups of five. Count the rest of the tally marks one by one.

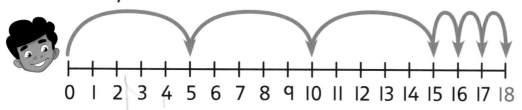

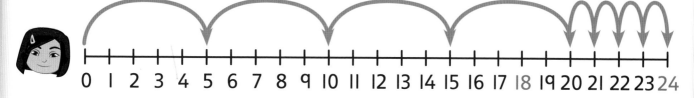

> The fifth tally mark is drawn across like this ꟷ.

Tariq won 18 games and Amy won 24 games.

b)

Tariq	ꟷ ꟷ ꟷ |||
Amy	ꟷ ꟷ ꟷ ꟷ ||||

> We can make it easier to find the total by counting in 5s.

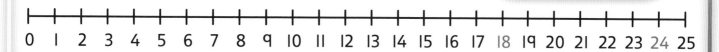

Amy won overall. 24 is greater than 18.

Think together

1 These choices have been tallied in a **tally chart**.

Write the tally number for each choice.

Choice	Tally	Number
✊	⅟⅟⅟⅟ ⅟⅟⅟⅟ |||	13
✋	⅟⅟⅟⅟ ⅟⅟⅟⅟ ||||	14
✌	⅟⅟⅟⅟ ⅟⅟⅟⅟ ||	12

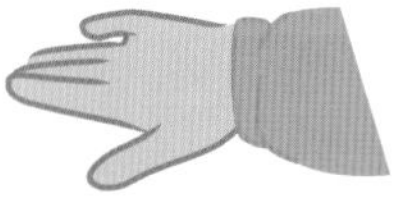

2 More children play the game. Here are the results.

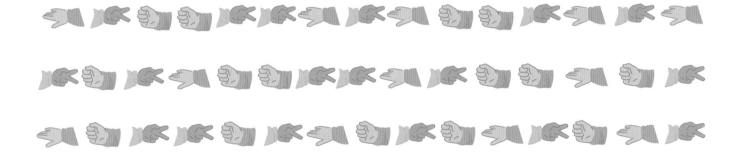

a) Create a tally chart to show how many of each is shown.

b) Which choice was the most popular?

Which choice was the least popular?

3 Tariq and Amy play another game of 'Rock, Paper, Scissors'.

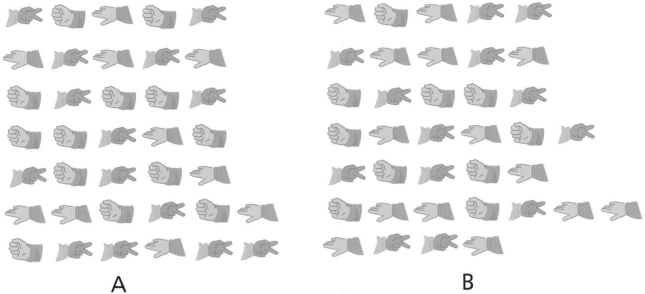

A   B

Which results does this table show? How do you know?

Choice	Tally	Number
![fist]	ⅢⅢ ⅢⅢ ‖‖	13
![hand]	ⅢⅢ ⅢⅢ	10
![scissors]	ⅢⅢ ⅢⅢ ‖‖‖	14

51

→ Practice book 2B p35

Creating pictograms ①

Discover

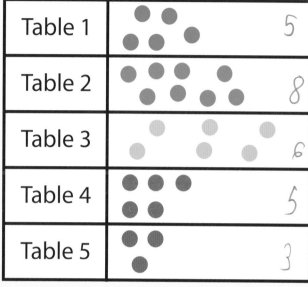

Table 1		5
Table 2		8
Table 3		6
Table 4		5
Table 5		3

Each ○ represents 1 table point.

You win table points for:
– being tidy
– trying hard
– helping others.

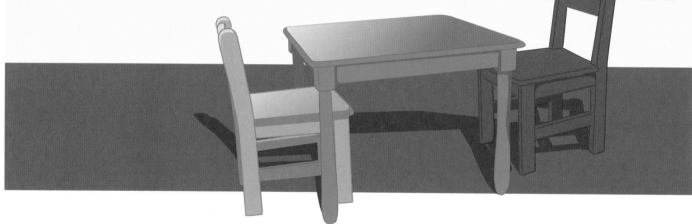

① **a)** Which table has the most points?

How could we make the points easier to count?

b) The children on table 3 get 3 more points.

How many stickers will they now have?

Share

a)

If we put the points in lines in a table we can make a **pictogram**.

Each ◯ represents I table point.

Table I	⬤ ⬤ ⬤ ⬤ ⬤
Table 2	⬤ ⬤ ⬤ ⬤ ⬤ ⬤ ⬤ ⬤
Table 3	◯ ◯ ◯ ◯ ◯ ◯
Table 4	⬤ ⬤ ⬤ ⬤ ⬤
Table 5	⬤ ⬤ ⬤

I will put the results into a tally chart to make them easier to count.

Every pictogram has to have a **key**. This tells us what each symbol represents.

Table 2 has the most points.

The children on table 2 have 8 points.

We can make a pictogram to make the points easier to count and compare.

Table	Tally	Number
Table I	卌	5
Table 2	卌 |||	8
Table 3	卌		6
Table 4	卌	5
Table 5	|||	3

b) The children on table 3 will now have 9 stickers.

Each ◯ represents 1 table point.

Table 1	●●●●●
Table 2	●●●●●●●●
Table 3	○○○○○○○○
Table 4	●●●●●
Table 5	●●●

Think together

Remember that a tally chart shows groups of five.

 a) Choose five animals and ask the children in your class: Which is your favourite animal?

b) Collect your results in a tally chart.

Animal	Tally	Number

2 Choose a symbol to represent the animals in your chart. Complete a pictogram to show your results.

Favourite animal	Number of children

3 **a)** Make a key for your pictogram.

Each ☐ represents ☐ animal.

b) Write a title for your pictogram.

A pictogram to show _____

_____

A pictogram has to have a key and a title.

55

Creating pictograms ❷

Discover

Each ◎ represents 5 hot dinners.

Day	Number
Monday	◎◎◎◎◎◎◎
Tuesday	◎◎◎◎◎
Wednesday	◎◎◎◎◎◎
Thursday	◎◎
Friday	

1 **a)** How many hot dinners were made on Tuesday?

b) 35 dinners are needed on Friday.

How many ◯ do you need to draw?

Share

a)

> I looked at the key. That is important.

Tuesday has 5 ◯ .

Each ◯ equals 5 hot dinners.

5 groups of 5 is equal to 25 hot dinners.

25 hot dinners were made on Tuesday.

b) 7 groups of 5 is equal to 35 hot dinners.

Each ◉ represents 5 hot dinners.

Friday	

I need to draw 7 ◯ .

> I wonder why we do not draw one ◯ for each dinner.

Think together

1   Ask the children in your class: How do you travel to school?

a) Collect your results in a tally chart.

Transport	Tally	Number
car		
bus		
bike		
walk		
other		

b) Which way of travelling to school was the most popular?

Which way of travelling to school was the least popular?

I wonder if I could use a pictogram instead of a tally chart.

2 Now complete a pictogram to show your results.

Use a  to represent the children.

Give your pictogram a title and a key.

This is a pictogram to show _____

_____ .

Each 😊 represents 2 children.

Transport	Number
car	
bus	
bike	
walk	
other	

3 **a)** What is the difference between the most and least popular way of getting to school?

CHALLENGE

b) How many children travel in a car or walk to school altogether?

→ Practice book 2B p41

Interpreting pictograms ❶

Discover

crab

Each ● represents I creature.

razor shell

sea snail

starfish

shrimp

Creature	Number of creatures
	●●●●
	●●●●●●●●
	●●●●●●
	●●
	●●●●●●●●●●

❶ **a)** Some children make a pictogram to show how many creatures they have found.

The labels are missing from the pictogram.

Work out where each label should go.

b) Which creature did the children find the most of?

Share

a) First we count how many of each creature there are.

Creature	Tally
crab	////
sea snail	##H ///
shrimp	##H /
razor shell	//
starfish	##H ##H

Then we complete the pictogram.

Each ● represents one creature.

Creature	Number of creatures
crab	●●●●
sea snail	●●●●●●●●
shrimp	●●●●●●
razor shell	●●
starfish	●●●●●●●●●●

b) There were 10 .

The creature the children found most of was .

Think together

1 Which creature did the children find the least of?

Creature	Number of creatures
crab	● ● ● ●
sea snail	● ● ● ● ● ● ● ●
shrimp	● ● ● ● ● ●
razor shell	● ●
starfish	● ● ● ● ● ● ● ● ● ●

The creature the children found the least of was _____ .

2 How many fewer are there than ?

☐ – ☐ = ☐

There are ☐ fewer 🦀 .

3 Complete the sentences.

There are ☐ more 🐚 than | .

There are 2 fewer _____ than ⭐ .

4 Four more 🦐 were seen on the beach.

Some more 🔪 were also seen.

There is now the same amount of both.

How many more 🔪 were seen?

CHALLENGE

> I am going to work out how many 🦐 there are now.

> I drew this bar model to help me.

shrimps	6	4

razor shells	2	

▢ more 🔪 were seen.

→ Practice book 2B p44

Interpreting pictograms ❷

Discover

Each 🐦 represents 5 birds.

Bird	Number
blackbird	🐦 🐦 🐦
robin	🐦 🐦
sparrow	🐦
blue tit	🐦 🐦 🐦 🐦

1 **a)** How many of each bird were seen?

b) Why does each 🐦 represent 5 birds?

Why don't we draw 1 🐦 for each bird?

Share

a) Each is worth 5.

15 blackbirds were seen.

10 robins were seen.

5 sparrows were seen.

20 blue tits were seen.

I used multiplication to find the number of birds.

There are 4  for blue tits.

Each  is worth 5.

4 groups of 5 equals 20 blue tits.

$4 \times 5 = 20$ blue tits.

b) We have drawn I ![bird icon] for 5 birds, like this.

Bird	Number
blackbird	![bird] ![bird] ![bird]

Each ![bird icon] being worth 5 birds makes it easier to count and quicker to draw.

There would be too many ![bird icon] if each one represented I bird, like this.

Bird	Number
blackbird	![bird] ![bird] ![bird] ![bird] ![bird] ![bird] ![bird] ![bird] ![bird] ![bird] ![bird] ![bird] ![bird] ![bird] ![bird]

Think together

I How many more blackbirds were seen than sparrows?

$\boxed{} - \boxed{} = \boxed{}$

There are $\boxed{}$ more blackbirds.

Bird	Number
blackbird	![bird] ![bird] ![bird]
robin	![bird] ![bird]
sparrow	![bird]
blue tit	![bird] ![bird] ![bird] ![bird]

2 10 more robins were seen.

How many more 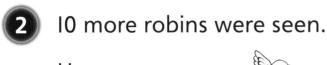 are needed in the pictogram?

☐ more  are needed in the pictogram.

3 After 10 more robins were seen, Mara drew a different pictogram for the same birds.

CHALLENGE

This time, each 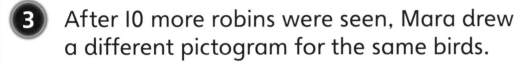 represents 10 birds.

Copy and complete Mara's pictogram.

I will think about how many birds each  represents.

Bird	Number
blackbird	
robin	
sparrow	
blue tit	

Can you explain to your partner what the 🐦 means?

→ Practice book 2B p47

Block diagrams

Discover

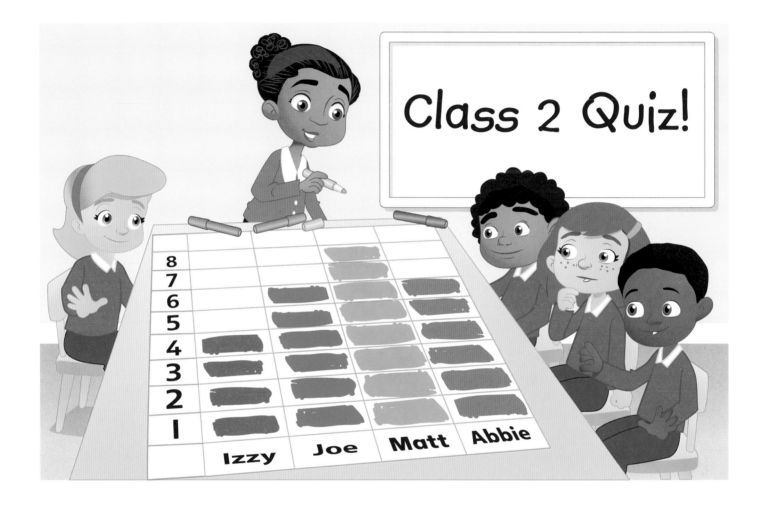

1 **a)** Who has the most points?

How do you know?

b) Which children have the same number of points?

How do you know?

Share

a) Count each score in 1s.

We could use cubes to help us!

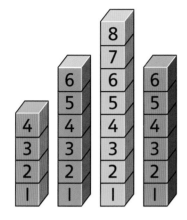

Izzy	4
Joe	6
Matt	8
Abbie	6

Use the scale on the side and compare the height of the towers.

This is called a block diagram.

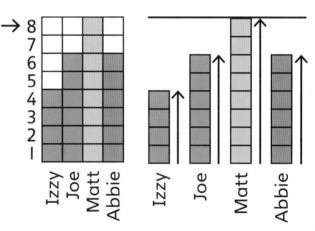

Matt has the most points as he has the highest tower.

b) Use cubes to see which towers are the same height.

Use the scale on the side and compare the heights of each tower to see which scores are the same.

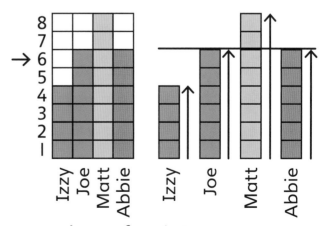

Joe and Abbie have the same number of points as the heights of their towers are the same.

Think together

1 The children in Class 2 are put into teams for a quiz.

Here are the results.

a) Which team scored the most points?

How do you know?

Team ☐ scored the most points.

b) Which team scored the least points?

How do you know?

Team ☐ scored the least points.

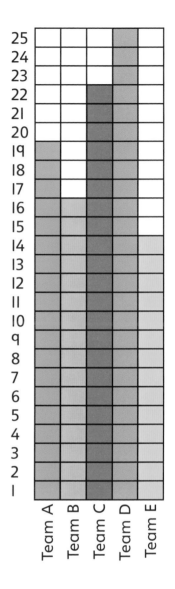

2 Use cubes to make a block diagram of these sports day team results.

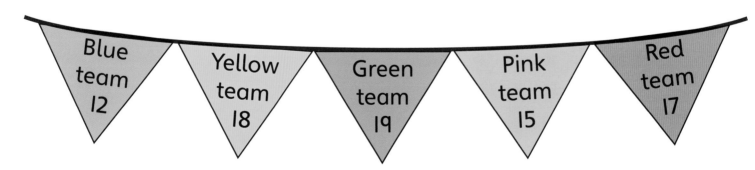

70

3 Three children are discussing favourite animals.

CHALLENGE

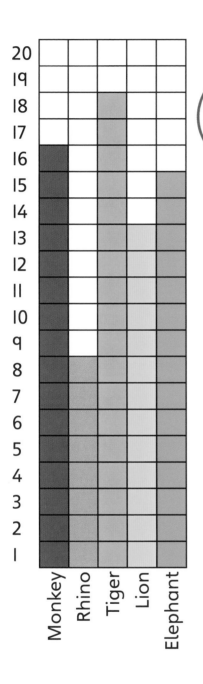

| | Monkey | Rhino | Tiger | Lion | Elephant |

The most popular animal is the tiger.

5 fewer children prefer the elephant to the tiger.

8 more children prefer the monkey to the rhino.

a) Are all the children correct?

b) Create your own question for this block diagram.

→ Practice book 2B p50

Solving word problems

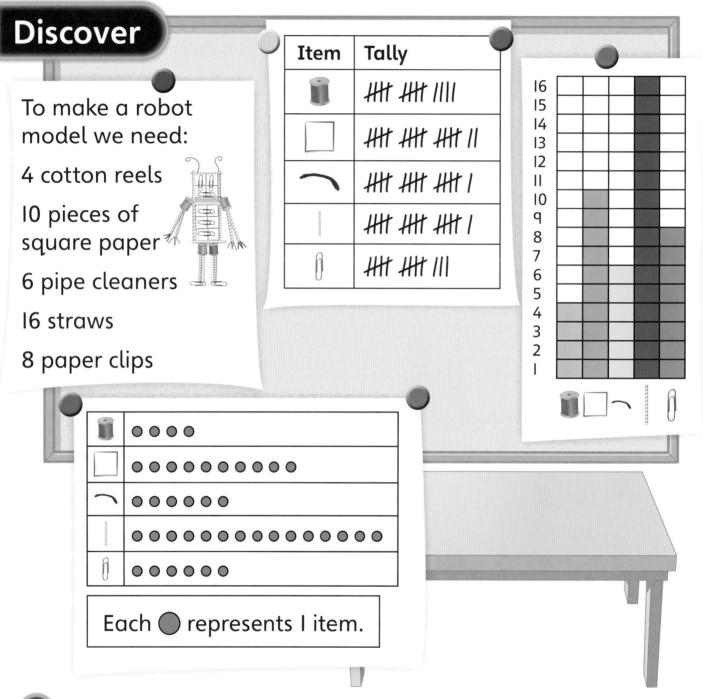

Discover

To make a robot model we need:

4 cotton reels

10 pieces of square paper

6 pipe cleaners

16 straws

8 paper clips

Item	Tally
🧵	ЖЖ ЖЖ ////
☐	ЖЖ ЖЖ ЖЖ //
⌒	ЖЖ ЖЖ ЖЖ /
│	ЖЖ ЖЖ ЖЖ /
📎	ЖЖ ЖЖ ///

Each ⬤ represents 1 item.

1 **a)** Which diagram correctly represents the model robot?

Only one diagram is correct.

b) What information is missing from the pictogram?

72

Share

a) There aren't enough straws or paper clips on the pictogram.

Each ⬤ represents I item.

There are too many cotton reels, pieces of paper, pipe cleaners and paper clips on the tally chart.

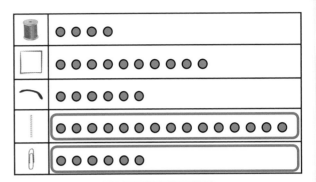

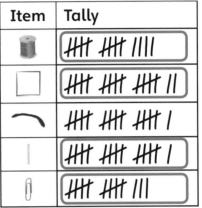

The block graph correctly represents the model robot because it matches the list of items needed.

b) The robot model needs 4 cotton reels, I0 pieces of paper, 6 pipe cleaners, I6 straws and 8 paper clips.

On the pictogram there are only I5 straws and 6 paper clips.

2 paper clips and I straw are missing.

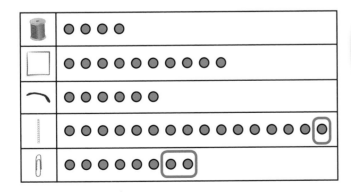

I will add 2 paper clips and I straw.

73

Think together

1 Here are the items needed for another robot.

Item	Tally
![spool]	卌
☐	卌 卌 卌
▮	卌 ‖
⌒	卌 ‖‖
⌐	卌 卌 ‖

a) How many more are needed than 🧵 ?

☐ – ☐ = ☐

☐ more are needed than 🧵 .

b) How many pieces are needed altogether?

2 Show the information on a block diagram.

3 Use the information to complete the diagrams.

CHALLENGE

Each ■ represents 2 of each item.

Item	Tally
☐	
▯	
⌒	
✂	

☐	■ ■
▯	
⌒	■ ■ ■ ■ ■
✂	

10
q
8
7
6
5
4
3
2
1

  ▯ ⌒ ✂

→ **Practice book 2B p53**

End of unit check

Your teacher will ask you these questions.

1 Which tally chart shows the correct amount of flowers?

red   blue   yellow   pink   orange

A

Flower	Tally
red 🌷	⳹ //
blue 🌸	///
yellow 🌼	⳹ //
pink 🌹	⳹ ////
orange 🌺	⳹ ///

C

Flower	Tally
red 🌷	⳹ /
blue 🌸	////
yellow 🌼	⳹ //
pink 🌹	⳹ ⳹
orange 🌺	⳹ ///

B

Flower	Tally
red 🌷	⳹ /
blue 🌸	⳹
yellow 🌼	⳹ //
pink 🌹	⳹ ///
orange 🌺	⳹ ///

D

Flower	Tally
red 🌷	⳹
blue 🌸	////
yellow 🌼	⳹ /
pink 🌹	⳹ ⳹
orange 🌺	⳹ ///

2 How many red apples are there?

- **A** $4\frac{1}{2}$
- **B** 45
- **C** 5
- **D** 50

green	🍏 🍏 🍏 🍏 🍏
red	🍎 🍎 🍎 🍎 🍎
pink	🍑 🍑 🍑

Each 🍎 represents 10 apples.

3 Which statement below is true?

A There are 6 red tractors.

B There are 7 more blue tractors than yellow tractors.

C There are double the amount of orange tractors than yellow tractors.

D There are 8 blue tractors.

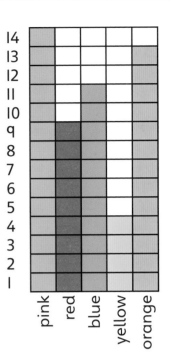

Think!

Each  represents 5 cars.

blue	🚐 🚐 🚐 🚐 🚐
red	🚐 🚐 🚐 🚐
yellow	🚐 🚐
purple	🚐 🚐 🚐 🚐

Today I saw more purple cars than red cars.

Is Ola correct? Explain your answer.

Create your own sentences about this pictogram.

These words might help you.

equal   **more than**   **less than**

most   **least**   **same as**

difference   **total**

77

→ Practice book 2B p56

Unit 8
Length and height

In this unit we will ...
- ⚡ Measure objects in centimetres and metres
- ⚡ Compare two lengths
- ⚡ Put lengths in order
- ⚡ Solve word problems about length

We will be using rulers.
How long is this piece of string?

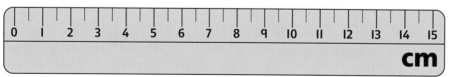

Here are some maths words we have seen before. Which ones mean the same thing?

length   centimetres   cm

metres   m   longer   shorter

metre sticks   height   width

compare   distance

We can also use a number line to compare lengths. Which straw is longer? What is the difference between them?

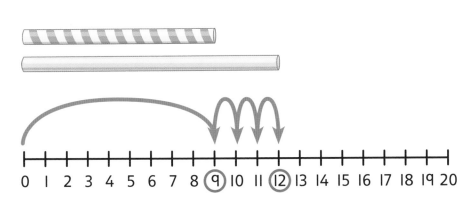

0   1   2   3   4   5   6   7   8   ⑨   10   11   ⑫   13   14   15   16   17   18   19   20

Measuring in centimetres

Discover

length	object
5 cm	
10 cm	
17 cm	
20 cm	
22 cm	

1 **a)** Kara and James are finding objects to match the lengths on the list. Which length would the ✏ be?

b) Which items measure 5 centimetres?

Share

a)

I am going to use a ruler to measure the length of the ✏.

The ✏ is exactly 10 cm long.

b) The items that look half this size are 5 cm long.

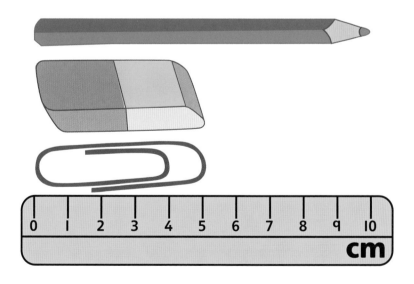

The ▱ and the ⤴ are 5 cm long.

Think together

 a) How long is the 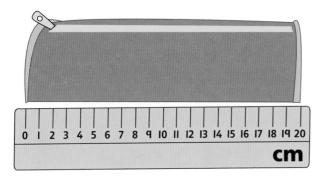 ?

The pencil case is ☐ cm long.

These rulers are not real rulers, so the centimetres are not quite the correct length.

b) How tall is the tower of ⬚ ?

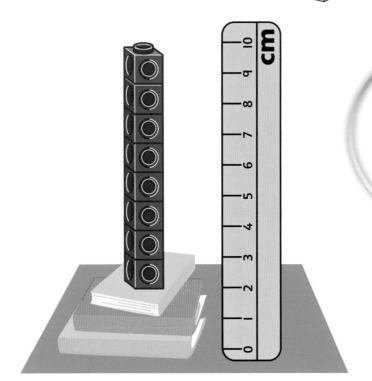

The tower is ☐ cm tall.

The tower is not on zero. I will count the centimetres, starting from 2 cm.

2 Find and measure something that is longer than the

 .

Find and measure something that is shorter than the

tower of .

longer than 20 cm	shorter than 8 cm

3 Which string is longer?

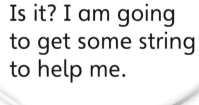

CHALLENGE

The straight string is clearly longer.

Is it? I am going to get some string to help me.

83

→ Practice book 2B p58

Measuring in metres

Discover

I wonder if the bus will fit in my classroom.

We can use these **metre** sticks to measure.

1 **a)** How will Kara and Tariq find out if the classroom is long enough to fit a 🚌 inside?

b) What other information do they need to see if the 🚌 will fit inside the classroom?

Share

a)

I know that a metre stays the same length anywhere in the world.

The bus is 12 metres long. I will find out the length of the classroom to see which is longer.

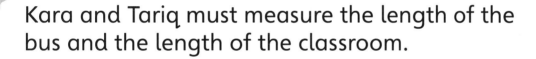

Kara and Tariq must measure the length of the bus and the length of the classroom.

b)

We need to know the height and width of our classroom.

The height of the bus is 5 metres.

The width of the bus is 3 metres.

Think together

1 **a)** The tallest man ever to live was nearly 3 metres tall. Would he fit through your classroom door?

b) The world record for the triple jump is over 18 metres. Would your school hall be long enough?

c) How far do you walk to get from your classroom to the hall?

A 1 metre stick is not long enough. I wonder if I could use a ball of string to help me.

2 Compare these distances. Use <, > or =.

a) 2 metres ◯ 20 metres

b) 9 metres ◯ 9 centimetres

c) 100 centimetres ◯ 1 metre

I wonder how we can check how many centimetres are in 1 metre.

CHALLENGE

3 Measure the height of things in your school playground.

Sort the things into groups of shorter than 1 metre and taller than 1 metre.

shorter than 1 metre	taller than 1 metre

I think I only need a 1 metre stick to check.

87

Comparing lengths

Discover

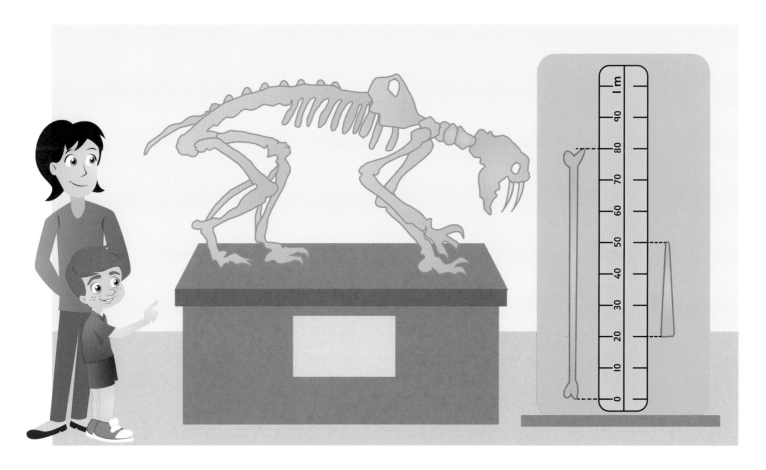

1 **a)** How long is ?

b) Which is bone is longer?

Share

a)

I counted up from 20 to 50. The difference was 30.

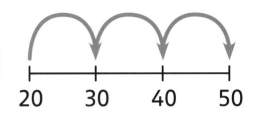

I moved the bone to the start of the ruler.

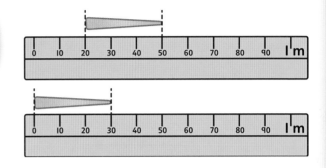

is 30 cm long.

b)

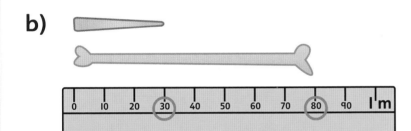

T	O

T	O

There are more tens in 80 than 30.

The ⟨bone⟩ is 80 cm long.

80 is greater than 30   80 > 30

30 is less than 80   30 < 80

The ⟨bone⟩ is longer than the ⟨⟩.

Think together

1 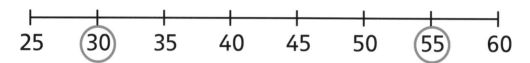 is 55 cm. Which bone is shorter,

_____ or _____ ?

| | 25 | 30 | 35 | 40 | 45 | 50 | 55 | 60 |

 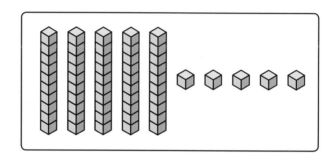

"I will compare the tens."

"You can use a number line to help you compare."

30 is _____ than 55.

30 ◯ 55

The _____ bone is shorter.

Thigh bone ⟞━━━━⟝

Shin bone ⟝━━━━⟞

Leg bone ◁━━━

90

2 Use <, > or = to compare these amounts.

a)

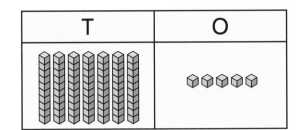 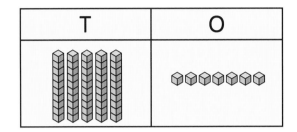

b)

20 cm ◯ 2 m

c)

50 cm ◯

---

3 Daisy has an object that is 40 cm tall.

Find and measure three things taller than it and three things smaller than it.

CHALLENGE

My ruler only goes up to 30 cm. I wonder if there is something else I can use.

91

→ **Practice book 2B p64**

Ordering lengths

Discover

Activities	Distances
Kicking football	25 metres
Jumping	7 metres
Throwing	16 metres

① **a)** Order the three distances from shortest to longest.

b) Work out the difference between the longest and shortest distance.

Share

I placed on a number line.

a)

0	7 metres	16 metres	25 metres

I compared the tens and ones in place value grids.

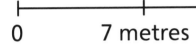

T	O
	🔲🔲🔲🔲🔲🔲🔲

T	O
▮	🔲🔲🔲🔲🔲🔲

T	O
▮▮	🔲🔲🔲🔲🔲

From shortest to longest, the distances are 7 metres, 16 metres and 25 metres.

b) 7 is the smallest number and 25 is the greatest number.

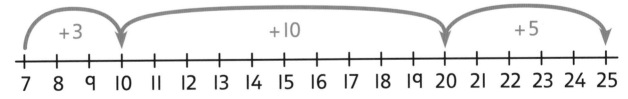

$7 + 18 = 25$

$25 - 18 = 7$

The difference between the longest and shortest distance is 18 metres.

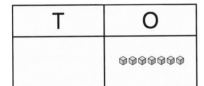

T	O
▮▮	🔲🔲🔲🔲🔲

T	O
▮▮	🔲🔲🔲🔲🔲 🔲🔲🔲🔲🔲 🔲🔲🔲🔲🔲

$$\begin{array}{r} \text{T} \quad \text{O} \\ {}^{1}\cancel{2} \ {}^{1}5 \\ - \ 1 \quad 8 \\ \hline 7 \end{array}$$

93

Think together

1 These are Nima's results.

Activities	Distances
Jumping	5 m
Throwing	12 m
Kicking football	20 m

Order them from greatest to smallest.

```
0                                        20
```

2 Martha kicked the football.

Her distance was greater than Jen's but smaller than Noah's.

How far could Martha have kicked the football?

Jen　　　　20 metres

Martha　?

Noah　　　25 metres

```
15                                  30
```

3 There are lots of things we can measure.

CHALLENGE

I could measure the length of our feet.

I could measure the length of our arms.

I could measure the length of our hair.

Pick one of these and measure everyone at your table.
Put the measurements in order from smallest to greatest.

Do we need to measure to compare the length of our arms?

95

→ Practice book 2B p67

Solving word problems – length

Discover

I **a)** How much string is there in total?

b) The string was cut from an 80 cm long piece.

How much string is left?

Share

a)

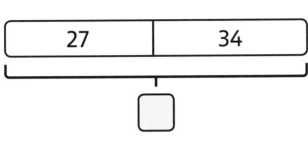

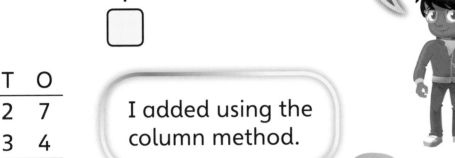

A bar model helped me to see it was adding.

```
   T  O
   2  7
+  3  4
   6  1
   1
```

I added using the column method.

$27 + 34 = 61$

There is 61 cm of string in total.

b)

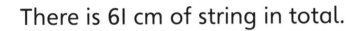

61   ?

80 cm

I used a number line and counted on.

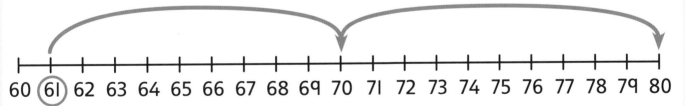

60 (61) 62 63 64 65 66 67 68 69 70 71 72 73 74 75 76 77 78 79 80

$80 - 61 = 19$

There is 19 cm of string left.

Think together

1 **a)** Aki has a 65 cm piece of string.

He uses 49 cm.

How much string is left?

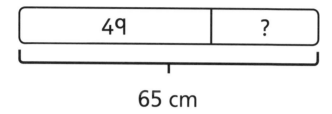

65 cm

65 − 49 = ☐

There is ☐ cm of string left.

b) A piece of string is cut into 3 pieces.

The first is 9 cm.

The second is 7 cm.

The final piece is 6 cm.

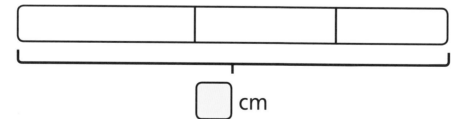

How long was the whole string?

☐ cm

☐ + ☐ + ☐ = ☐

The whole string was ☐ cm long.

2

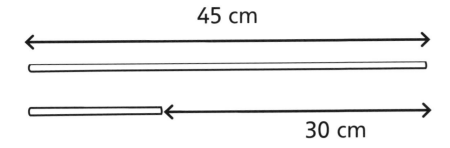

45 cm

30 cm

One piece of string is 45 cm long.

Another piece is 30 cm shorter.

How long is the other piece of string?

The other piece of string is ☐ cm long.

3 Two pieces of string are 34 cm long in total.

What could their lengths be?

CHALLENGE

I will pick a number smaller than 34 and then work out the difference.

First number: 20   Second number: ☐

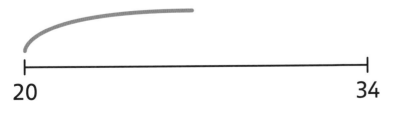

20   34

99

End of unit check

Your teacher will ask you these questions.

1. A toy car is 6 cm long. Which line shows the correct length?

A ————————————————

B ————————

C ——————————————————

D ——————————

2. Which unit is best for measuring the length of the school hall?

A Centimetres

B Metres

C Paper clips

D Kilograms

3. Which number sentence is incorrect?

A 1 m = 100 cm

B 50 cm > 40 cm

C 24 cm > 36 cm

D 60 cm > 55 cm

 Order these lengths starting with the shortest.

Which order is correct?

17 cm   8 m   2 cm

A 8 m, 17 cm, 2 cm   **C** 17 cm, 2 cm, 8 m

B 2 cm, 17 cm, 8 m   **D** 2 cm, 8 m, 17 cm

Think!

The pencil is 8 cm long.

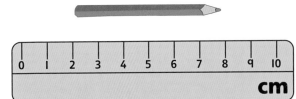

Is Hassan correct? Explain your answer.

These words might help you.

ruler   centimetre

metre

long   tall   short

101

→ Practice book 2B p73

Unit 9
Properties of shapes

In this unit we will ...
- ⚡ Recognise 2D and 3D shapes
- ⚡ Count the sides and vertices on 2D shapes
- ⚡ Learn about symmetry
- ⚡ Count the faces, edges and vertices on 3D shapes
- ⚡ Sort 2D and 3D shapes

How are these shapes similar?
How are they different?

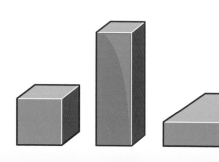

We need lots of words to describe 2D and 3D shapes. Do you know any of these words?

quadrilateral **polygon** **prism**

hexagon **octagon** **vertex** **vertices**

hemisphere **symmetry** **line of symmetry**

symmetrical **curved surface**

Do you remember what these are called?

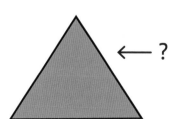 ← ?

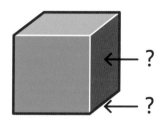 ← ?

← ?

Recognising 2D and 3D shapes

Discover

1 a) The children have made pictures using 2D shapes.

Which picture did Mia make?

b) Which picture did Sunil make?

Share

a) Mia's picture has two squares.

Which picture has two squares?

I think squares look like this ☐ .

No. That is a rectangle but not a square. A square is a rectangle where all the sides are the same length. Rectangles and squares are **quadrilaterals** because they have four sides.

This is Mia's picture.

b) This is Sunil's picture.

A triangle can be printed in different ways. Remember that a triangle that appears to be upside-down is still a triangle.

Think together

1 How many rectangles are there in this picture?

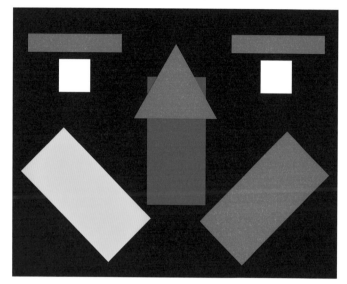

I can name other shapes in the picture.

There are ☐ rectangles in this picture.

2 Name the 3D shapes.

   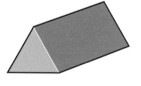

Which 3D shapes could you use to print the 2D shapes in the pictures?

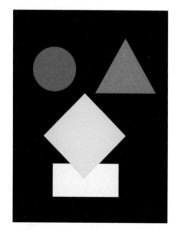 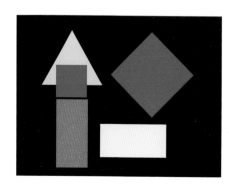 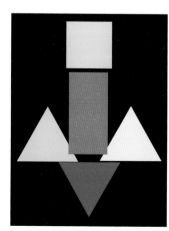

3 Ben draws a rectangle using a cuboid as a stencil.

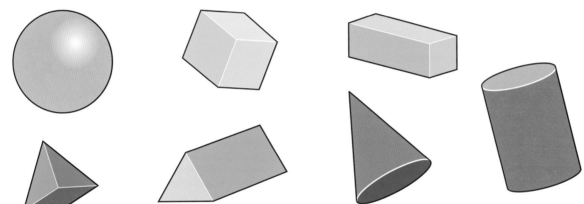

Which 2D shapes can you draw using these 3D shapes?

I will draw around all of these shapes.

107

→ Practice book 2B p75

Drawing 2D shapes

Discover

1 **a)** Draw a square accurately.

b) Draw a triangle accurately.

Share

a) To draw a square, you need four corners.

I will use squared paper and a ruler to help.

Work out where the corners should go.	Use your ruler to line up with two dots.	Start at one dot, then stop when you reach the next dot.

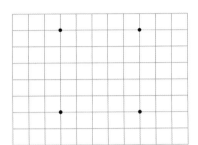 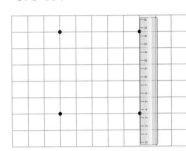 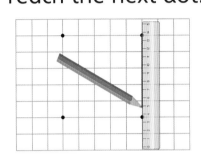

Draw all four sides of the square in the same way to complete your square.

I've drawn a square accurately.

b) To draw a triangle, you need three dots.

Put the dots on the grid lines and use your ruler to line up with two dots. Draw each side in this way.

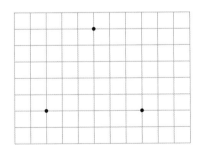 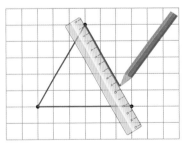

2D shapes drawn with only straight lines are called **polygons**.

I know these shapes are not polygons.

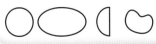

Think together

You will need to add more dots.

1   Copy these dots on squared paper.

Use them to draw two different rectangles.

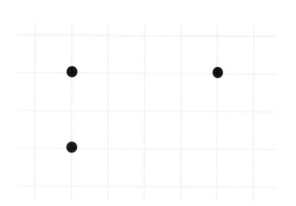

2   Copy these triangles.

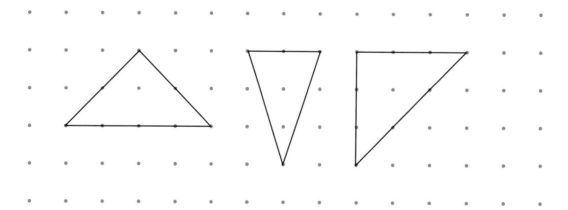

3 **a)** The dots in these shapes have been joined together.

Copy the shapes accurately on squared paper.

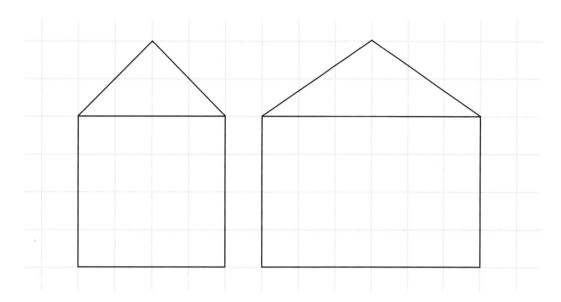

b) Now try drawing these shapes on plain paper.

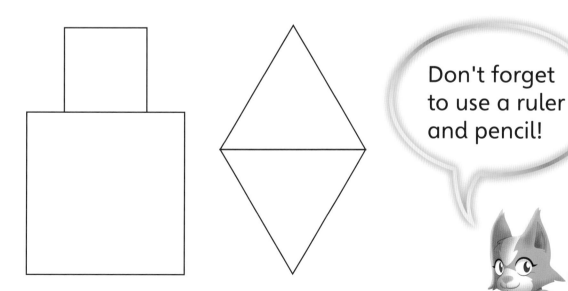

Don't forget to use a ruler and pencil!

III

Counting sides on 2D shapes

Discover

1 **a)** Jess wants to use a different colour for each side of the shape.

   How many pens will she use for a 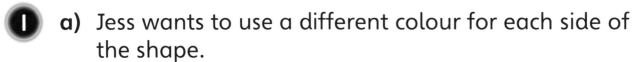 ?

   b) Does Jess have enough pens to draw the sides of each shape in a different colour?

Share

I will start by counting all the sides.

a)

A side is a straight line that joins two corners of a 2D shape.

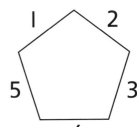

side

This shape has five sides.

A shape with five sides is called a **pentagon**.

Jess will use five different coloured pens for a ⬠ .

b) Jess has five pens.

I can draw these shapes with different coloured sides.

A ⬡ has six sides.

A shape with six sides is called a **hexagon**.

Jess does not have enough pens to draw each side of a ⬡ in a different colour.

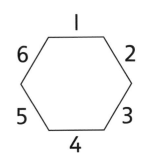

Think together

1

I wonder if there are other quadrilaterals.

Kat only wants to draw quadrilateral shapes.

Which shapes should she draw?

2 Milo is making shapes using sticks.

How many sides does each shape have?

 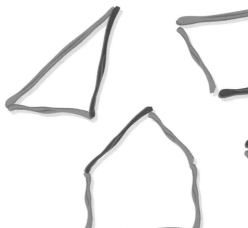 

3 Count the sides of each shape.

How many shapes are quadrilaterals?

CHALLENGE

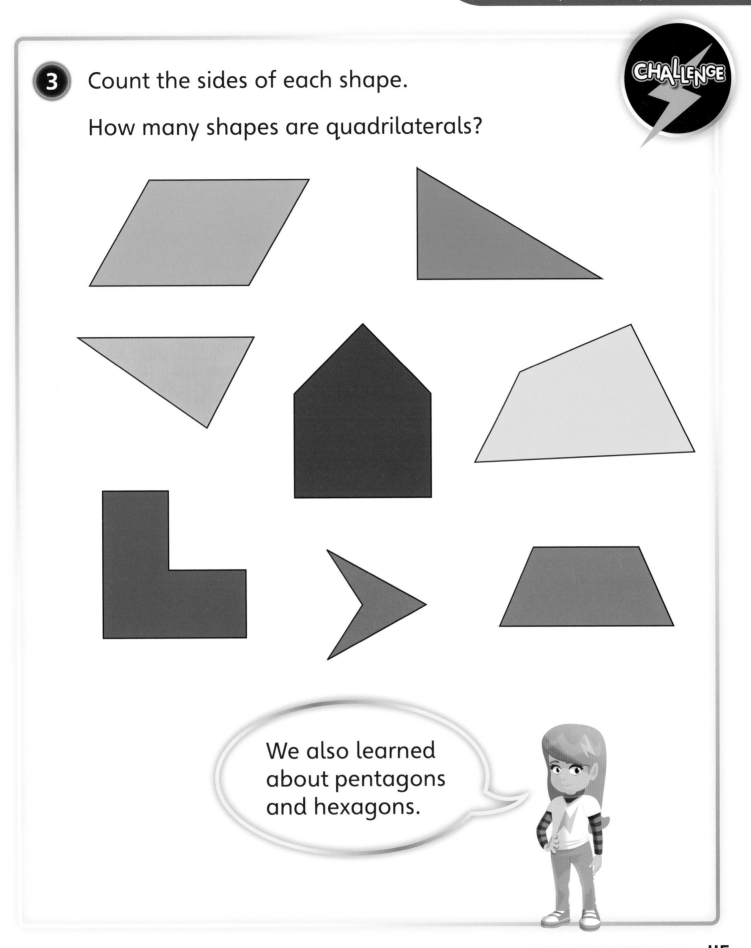

We also learned about pentagons and hexagons.

115

Counting vertices on 2D shapes

Discover

1 a) How many fingers are needed to make a ⬜ ?

How many fingers are needed for a ⬠ ?

b) How many different shapes can you make using three fingers?

Share

a) A square needs four fingers because it has four corners.

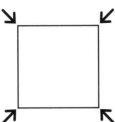

The accurate name for a corner is a **vertex**. The plural is **vertices**.

To make a ⬠ I need to count how many vertices it has.

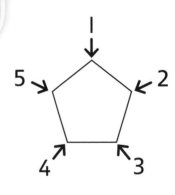

There are five vertices on a ⬠ so the children need to use five fingers.

b)

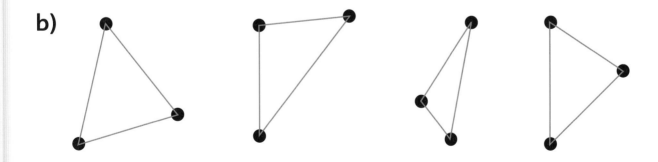

The only shape you can make with three fingers is a triangle. It has three vertices.

Think together

1 Count the number of vertices on each shape.

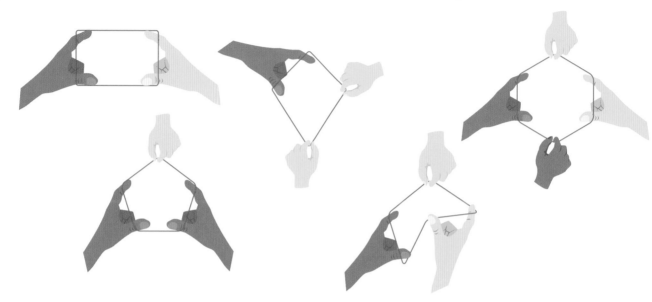

2 Count the number of vertices on each shape.

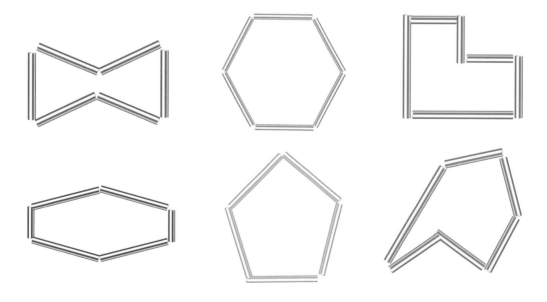

I know that a six-sided shape is called a hexagon.

3

CHALLENGE

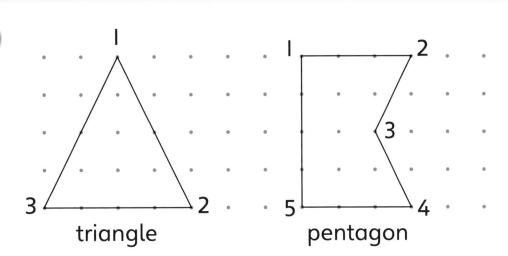

triangle   pentagon

A triangle has three sides and three vertices. A pentagon has five sides and five vertices.

Count the number of sides and vertices of these shapes.

A   B   C

   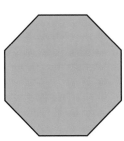

☐ sides   ☐ sides   ☐ sides
☐ vertices   ☐ vertices   ☐ vertices

119

→ Practice book 2B p84

Finding lines of symmetry

Discover

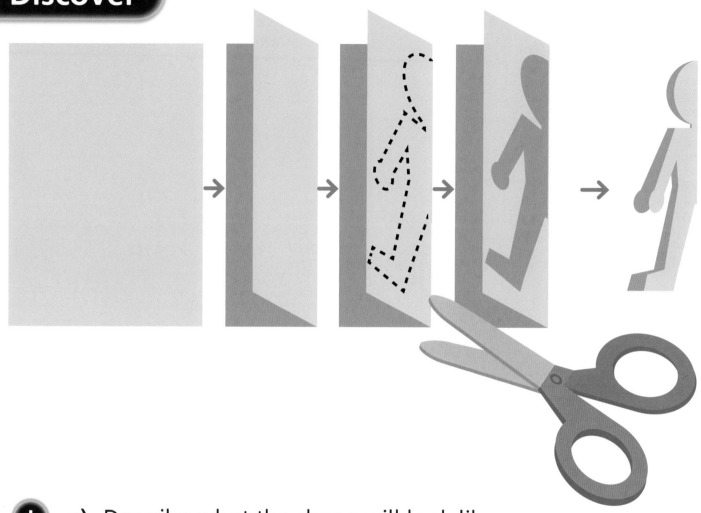

1 a) Describe what the shape will look like when it is unfolded.

b) What will this shape look like when it is unfolded?

Share

a)

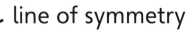

line of symmetry

> The line between the two halves is called the **line of symmetry**.

> When the paper is folded on the line of symmetry, the two parts match exactly. The shape is **symmetrical**.

The shape will look like a person when it is unfolded.

b) This shape is symmetrical too.

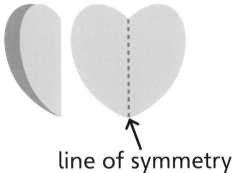

line of symmetry

The shape will look like a heart when it is unfolded.

> I think you can use a mirror to see that it is symmetrical.

Think together

1   What will these shapes look like when they are unfolded?

2   Complete the symmetrical shapes.

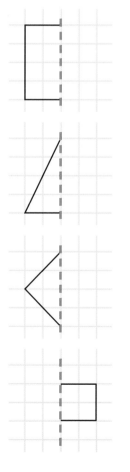

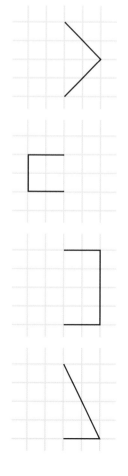

I will check using a mirror.

3 Which lines of symmetry are correct?

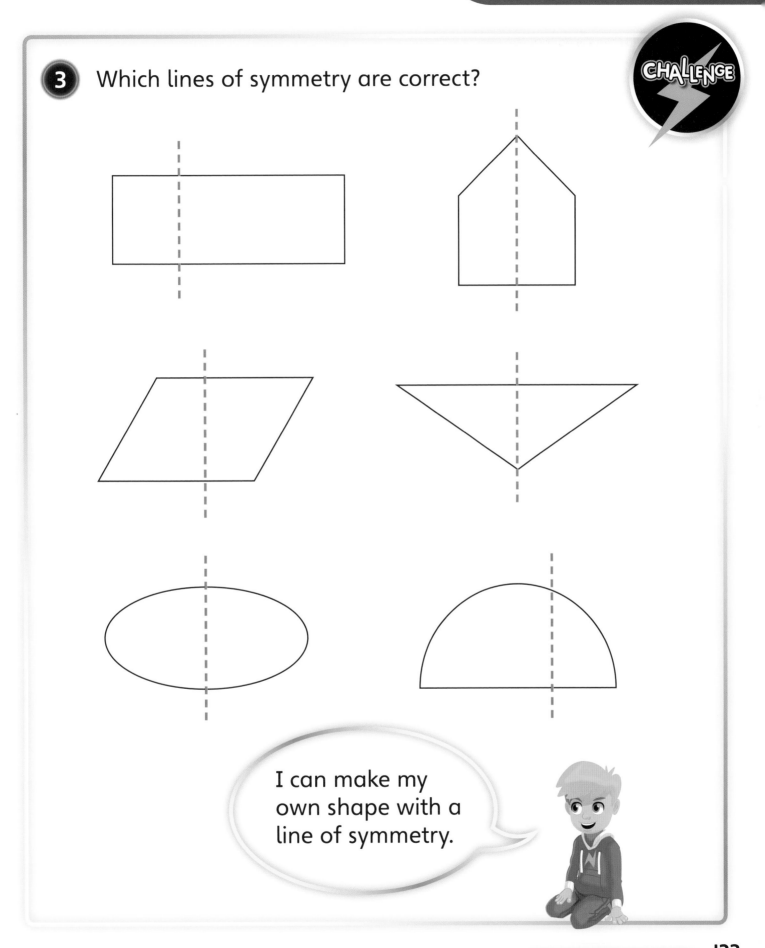

CHALLENGE

I can make my own shape with a line of symmetry.

123

Sorting 2D shapes

Discover

1 **a)** Which shape will **not** go in either box?

b) Which shape has the most vertices?

Share

a) These shapes have all got blue stripes so they go in this box.

Blue stripy shapes

> I want to make sure about this shape . It has blue stripes, but it also has a lot of vertices.

> It has five vertices, but the shapes have to have **more** than five to go in the other box.

These shapes have more than five vertices so they go in this box.

Shapes with more than 5 vertices

This shape does not have blue stripes and it does not have more than five vertices.

The yellow triangle will not go in either box.

b) This shape 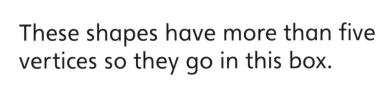 has six vertices. It is called a hexagon.

This shape has eight vertices. It is called an **octagon**.

Eight is greater than six (8 > 6).

The red octagon has the most vertices.

> These shapes have more vertices than the other shapes.

125

Think together

1 What labels could go on these boxes?

I think a polygon is a 2D shape with straight sides.

I know that circles, ovals and semi-circles are not polygons because they all have curves.

2 Sort these shapes into order by number of sides, from the fewest number of sides to the most.

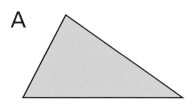

A

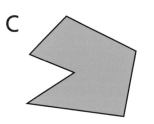

C

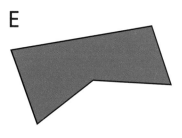

E

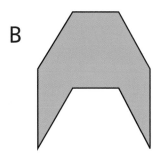

B

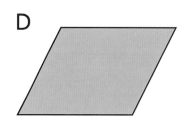

D

F

Fewest sides _____ Most sides

3 Think of your own ways of sorting these into two groups.

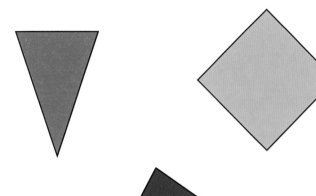

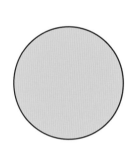

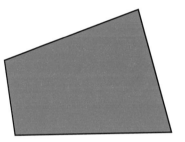

I thought of sorting them by symmetry.

There are lots of different ways. Has someone else thought of a different way to sort them?

127

→ Practice book 2B p90

Making patterns with 2D shapes

Discover

| 1 | 2 | 3 | 4 | 5 | 6 | 7 | 8 | 9 | 10 | 11 | 12 |

Complete the pattern using one of these options.

A: ◆▲   C: ◆ ●

B: ■ ●   D: ● ■

1 **a)** Which is the correct option to complete the pattern?

b) What shape would be in position 20?

Share

a) The options are A ,

B , C  and

D .

Four shapes are repeated to make the pattern.

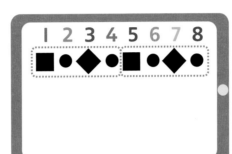

I know it cannot be **A** because there are no triangles in the pattern.

To work out the answer, find the part of the pattern that repeats. Then compare the repeating pattern to find the missing shapes.

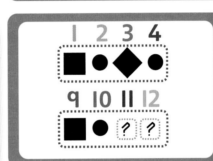

I will now compare the repeating part to find the missing shapes.

Option C  is correct.

b)

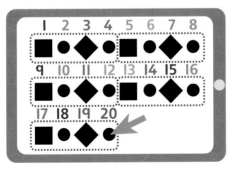

I can see that the even numbers always have a circle.

The 20th shape must be a circle.

Think together

1. Find the repeating parts to complete the pattern.

   What are the missing shapes?

I will first work out the part that repeats.

2. What shape will be in position 15?

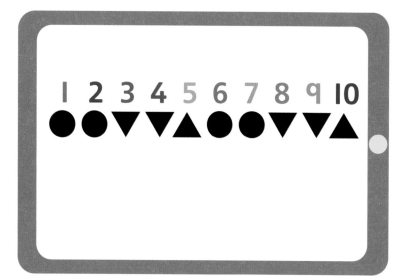

I will draw the pattern to position 15.

3 Describe each pattern to your partner.

Draw the missing shapes for each pattern.

a)

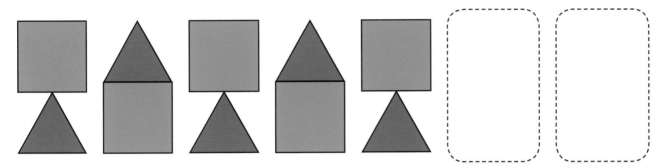

b)

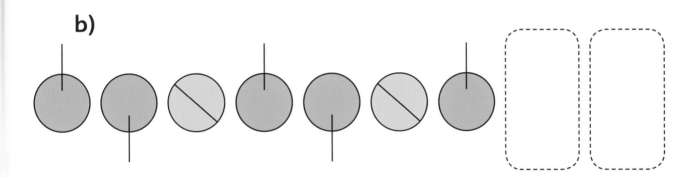

c)

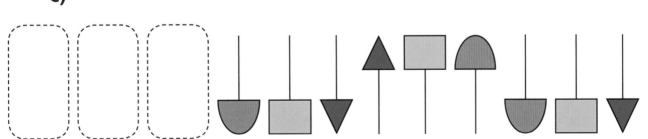

→ Practice book 2B p93

Counting faces on 3D shapes

Discover

1 **a)** Ben paints every face of the box a different colour.

How many colours will he need?

b) Describe the shape of each face.

Share

a)

A face is a flat surface on a 3D shape. Each face is a 2D shape.

A cuboid has three pairs of faces.

A cuboid has six faces in total.

1   2   3   4   5   6

Ben will need six different colours.

b) The shape of each face is a rectangle.

This 3D shape is a cuboid.

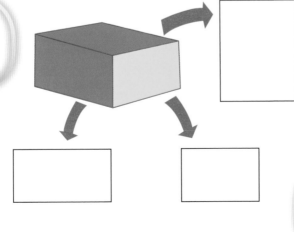

A cuboid can have two square faces.

Think together

1 How many faces does each shape have?

2 Anna wants to make a square-based pyramid from construction materials.

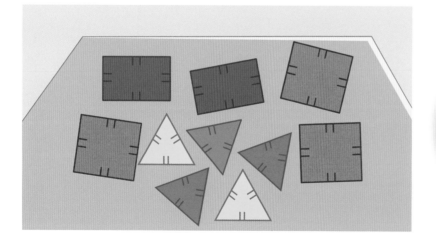

I know that some pyramids have a square base and some have a triangular base.

How many square faces does she need?

How many triangular faces does she need?

How many faces will there be in total?

CHALLENGE

3 How many faces does each shape have?

What shapes are the faces?

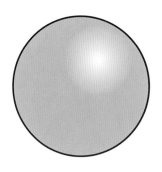 

A cone and a **hemisphere** have a circular face and a **curved surface**.

 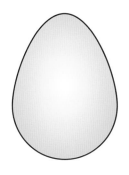 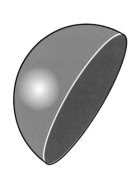

Does a sphere have a face? If I try to print using a sphere, I don't get a circle.

Remember, a face is a flat surface.

135

Counting edges on 3D shapes

Discover

Look at my bubble!

| Molly | Bob | Hassan |

1 **a)** Hassan wants to make his own 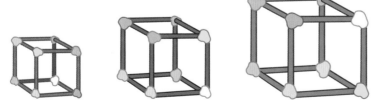.

How many ╱ does he need?

b) There are three different : small, medium and large.

What stays the same and what changes?

Share

a)

It looks like a cube but it doesn't have any faces. I wonder what it is.

I can only see the edges of the shape.

A 3D shape has **edges** where two faces meet.

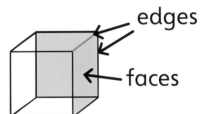

edges

faces

A cube has 12 edges.

In , there is one straw

for each edge.

Hassan needs 12 | to

make a .

I will count the edges in order, so I don't miss any edges or count any twice.

b)

  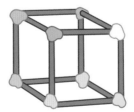

Each cube has six square faces and 12 edges. This stays the same.

The length of each edge changes and the size of each face changes.

Think together

1 Molly makes different shapes to dunk in the bubble mixture.

How many straws are needed to make each shape?

Shape	Number of straws needed

The last shape has a triangle at each end. It is called a triangular **prism**.

2 Sam has eight straws to make the edges of a 3D shape.

Which shapes can he make?

 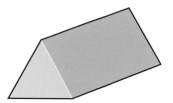 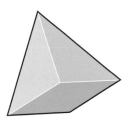 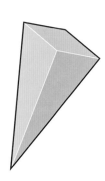

3 Malik and Abbie are making shapes from construction materials.

My cube has more edges than faces.

Does my pyramid have more faces or more edges?

Does a 3D shape always have more edges than faces?

I will investigate other shapes.

139

Counting vertices on 3D shapes

1 **a)** Eve is making a triangle-based pyramid.

How many  does she need?

b) How many more  does she need for this pyramid?

Share

a) Eve makes the base first.

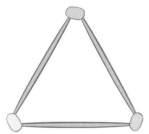

Eve uses three sticks and joins them at one vertex at the top.

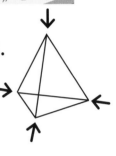

There is a  at each vertex.

A pyramid with a triangle base has four vertices.

Eve needs four  for this pyramid.

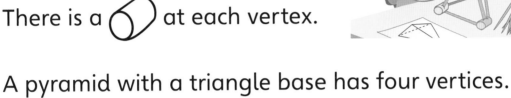

b) Eve makes a square base.

Then Eve makes one more vertex at the top point.

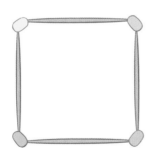

A pyramid with a square base has five vertices.

 needs four .

 needs five .

Eve needs one more for 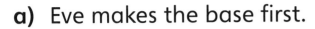.

Think together

1 How many vertices does each shape have?

Shape	Number of vertices

Remember there is a at each vertex.

2 George wants to make different pyramids.

Each pyramid has a different base.

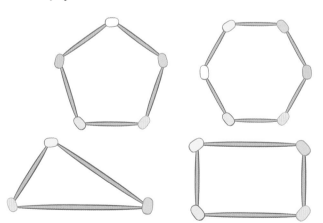

I know each pyramid will have a point as well as a base.

How many does George need for each pyramid?

3 Darcey has eight .

She joins them to make a 3D shape.

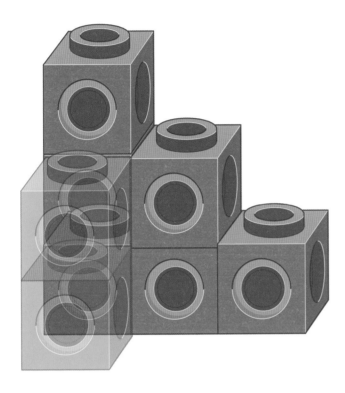

Can she make a shape with eight vertices?

Is there more than one solution?

143

→ Practice book 2B p102

Sorting 3D shapes

Discover

1 **a)** Which shapes are in the wrong place?

b) Can you think of a different shape that could go in both the 'Six faces' group and the 'Pyramids' group?

Share

I will check the shapes one by one.

a)

All cuboids have six faces so they need to be in this group.

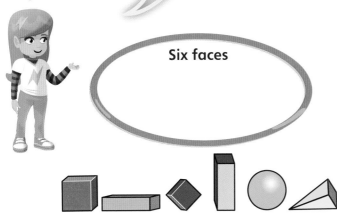

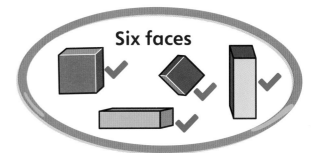

A sphere has one curved surface. It's not a pyramid so I think it should go in the 'Other' group.

This shape has five faces.

It is a pyramid.

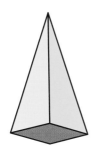

These shapes are not pyramids.

They should be in the 'Other' group.

It is a pyramid so it should go in the 'Pyramids' group.

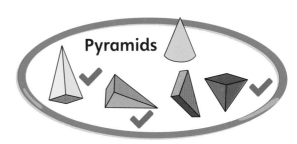

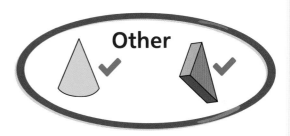

b)

To go in both the 'Six faces' and 'Pyramids' groups, the shape would need six faces and be a pyramid.

This shape has a five-sided base. It has five triangular faces and one face that is a pentagon.

It has six faces in total.

It could go in both groups.

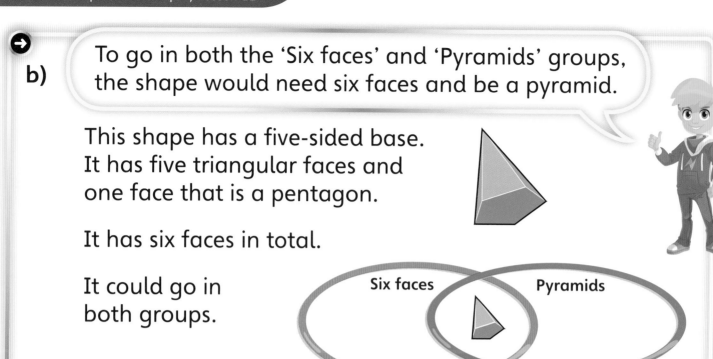

Six faces   Pyramids

Think together

1. Match the shapes to the number of edges.

< 10 edges   > 10 edges

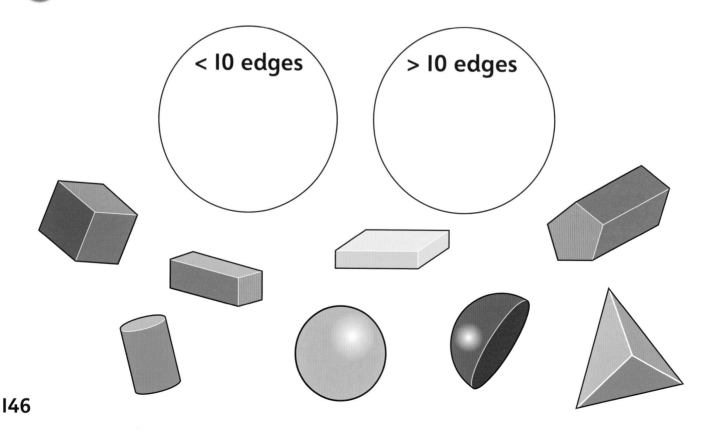

146

2 Put these shapes in order of the number of faces.

  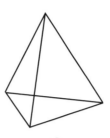  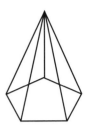

A B C D E

most faces _____ fewest faces

3 Choose headings to sort these shapes into three different groups.

I will make one of the headings about curved surfaces.

This reminds me of when we sorted 2D shapes.

147

→ Practice book 2B p105

Making patterns with 3D shapes

Discover

1 a) Describe the pattern of 3D shapes.

b) Create the same sort of pattern using these shapes.

Share

a)

> I wonder why this pattern doesn't repeat.

> I think it is a different kind of pattern.

The pattern is the same whether you start from the left or the right.

The matching shapes are in the same order from the middle.

It is a symmetrical pattern.

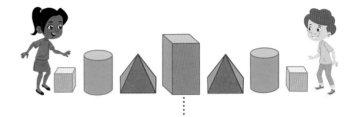

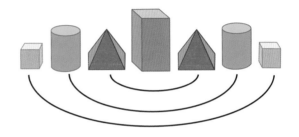

b) There is only one cylinder, so it must go in the middle.

Then there must be two matching shapes.

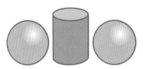

Then two more.

Then the last two.

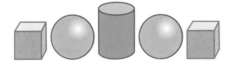

> Did you put the matching shapes in a different order?

Think together

1 Work out the missing shapes in these symmetrical patterns.

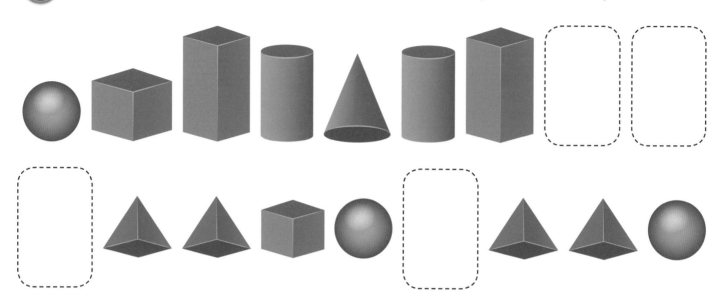

2 Create a symmetrical pattern with these sets of shapes.

a)

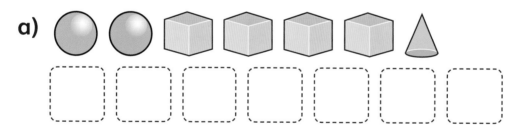

b)

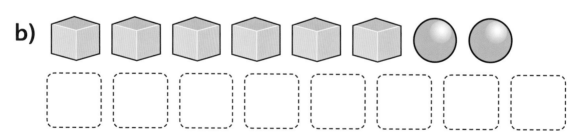

c)

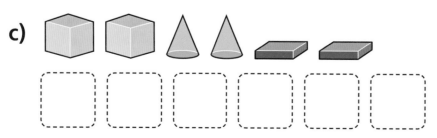

3 Can you make a symmetrical pattern with some of these shapes?

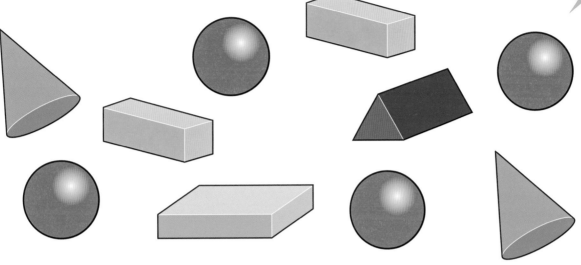

Can you also make a repeating pattern?

I wonder if there is more than one solution for each question.

I know I can make symmetrical patterns and repeating patterns with 3D shapes.

151

→ Practice book 2B p108

End of unit check

Your teacher will ask you these questions.

1 Which shape does not have four vertices?

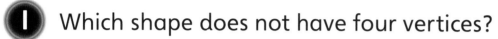

A   B   C   D

2 Which shape could not go in either group?

Pentagons   Even number of sides

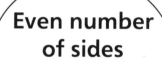

A   B   C   D

3 Choose the shape that has the fewest edges.

A   B   C   D

4 Which shape has these faces?

A   B   C   D

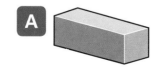

5 Choose the shape to complete the pattern

A rectangle   **B** square   **C** pentagon   **D** hexagon.

Think!

Theo has a square. He draws two straight lines on it and then cuts along them.

Now he has three new shapes.

He counts the number of vertices for each new shape.

Two of the shapes have three vertices.

One of the shapes has four vertices.

Find a way to cut the square into three shapes so each shape has a different number of vertices.

Is there more than one way? Describe your shapes to your partner.

These words might help you.

     vertices   **sides**

   pentagon   **hexagon**   **triangle**

153

→ Practice book 2B p111

Unit 10
Fractions

In this unit we will ...
- ⚡ Learn about the whole and equal parts
- ⚡ Recognise and find a half
- ⚡ Recognise and find a quarter
- ⚡ Learn about unit fractions
- ⚡ Count in halves and quarters

What is half of 6?

You can use ◯ to help.

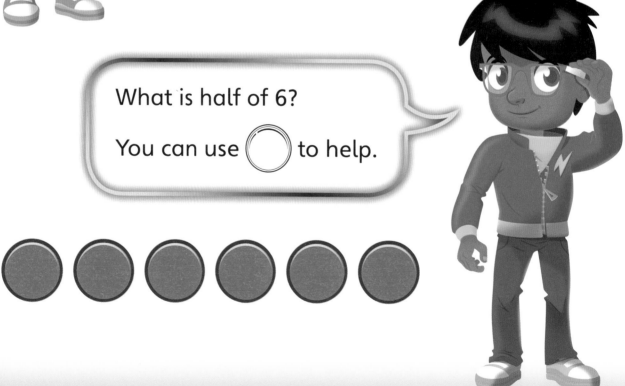

We will need some maths words. Some are new. Which words do you remember?

half ($\frac{1}{2}$)   quarter ($\frac{1}{4}$)   whole

third ($\frac{1}{3}$)   eqivalent

equal part   numerator

denominator   fraction bar

non-unit fraction

unit fraction

Which of these is the odd one out? Why?

Introducing whole and parts

Discover

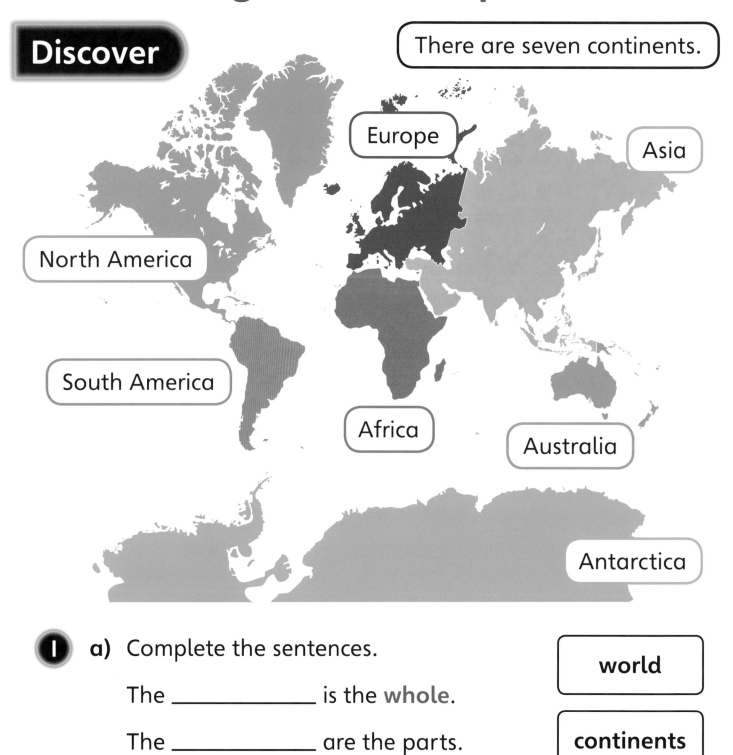

There are seven continents.

Europe

Asia

North America

South America

Africa

Australia

Antarctica

1 **a)** Complete the sentences.

The _____ is the **whole**.

The _____ are the parts.

world

continents

b) How many parts are there?

Share

a)

The world is the whole.   The continents are the parts.

The world is the whole. Europe is a part.

The world is the whole and Africa is a part.

I can make lots of sentences using the words whole and parts.

b) There are seven continents, so there are seven parts.

I wonder if the parts are **equal**?

157

Think together

1 Complete the sentences.

Here is the United Kingdom. There are four countries in the United Kingdom.

a) The _____ is the whole.

b) _____ is a part.

I think I can complete this in more than one way.

2 Here is an elephant.

Complete the sentences in different ways.

Use the words in the box.

| elephant |
| trunk |
| ear |
| tail |
| tusk |
| eye |

a) The _____ is the whole.

b) The _____ is a part.

3 Use the words 'whole' and 'part' to complete these sentences.

a)

The duck is the _____ .

The beak is a _____ .

b)

The sail is a _____ .

The boat is the _____ .

c)

The pizza is the _____ .

The cheese is a _____ .

→ Practice book 2B p113

Making equal parts

Discover

This is not fair.

1 **a)** Why is it not fair?

What could they have done differently?

b) Divide the cake fairly for four children.

Share

a)

I think the pieces are not equal.

Equal means the same.

It is not fair because one of the parts is bigger than the other.

They could have cut the cake into two **equal parts**.

b)

The cake has been cut into four equal parts.

Each child will get the same size piece.

Think together

1 Which show equal parts?

A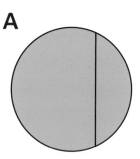

C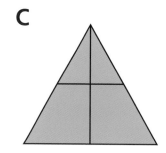

E

B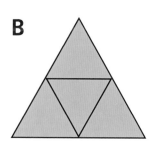

D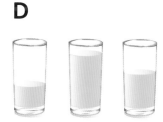

F

_____ show equal parts.

2 Which is the odd one out? Explain why.

A

B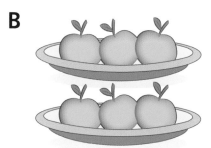

C

Complete this sentence.

The odd one out is because _____

_____ .

3 Make equal groups of children.

CHALLENGE

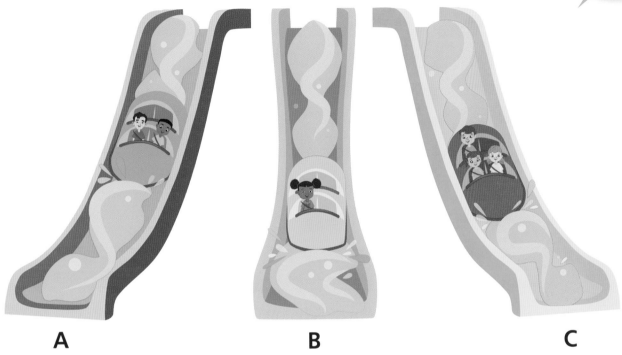

A   B   C

I think there is more than one way if I do not use all the boats.

163

Recognising a half ($\frac{1}{2}$)

Discover

1 **a)** What does $\frac{1}{2}$ mean?

   b) Which diagrams show halves?

   Which ones do not show halves?

Share

a) $\frac{1}{2}$ means I of 2 equal parts.

We read $\frac{1}{2}$ as a half.

It means we share equally between 2.

> I know that sharing equally between 2 is like dividing by 2.

$\frac{1}{2}$ is a **fraction**.

The **denominator** is the total number of equal parts.

$\frac{1}{2}$

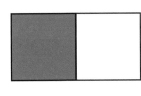

The **numerator** is how many equal parts we have.

The **fraction bar** goes between the numerator and the denominator.

b)

Halves	Not halves
☆	🥛
◑	🔺
▦▦	▦▦

Think together

1 Copy each shape.

Divide each shape into two equal parts.

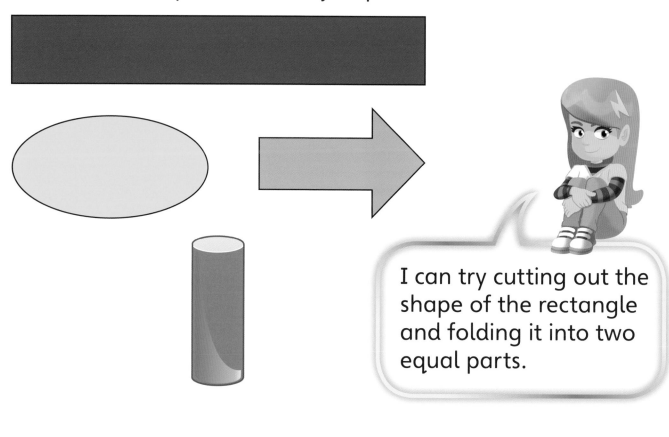

I can try cutting out the shape of the rectangle and folding it into two equal parts.

2 **a)** Copy each shape.

Shade half of each shape.

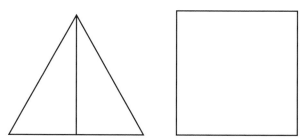

b) Here is half a shape.

What will the whole shape be?

3 **a)** Is this shape split into two equal parts?
Explain your answer.

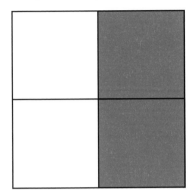

b) Is this shape split into two equal parts?
Explain your answer.

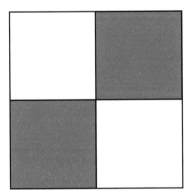

c) How many other ways can you split
this shape into two equal parts?

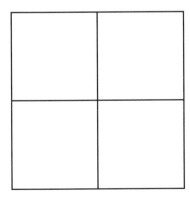

I wonder if $\frac{1}{2}$ always has to be equal parts?

167

→ **Practice book 2B p119**

Finding a half

Discover

1 a) Make two equal teams.

   b) Another player joins. Can the teams still be equal?

       Explain your answer.

Share

a) There are 12 players.

They need to be in two equal teams.

You can share the players one at a time.

There are 6 players in each team.

$\frac{1}{2}$ of 12 is 6.

Is that the same as $12 \div 2 = 6$?

Team A   Team B

b) 13 is an odd number.

Can I split an odd number into two equal parts?

The teams cannot be equal.

We need two more each time for the teams to be equal.

Think together

1 Find $\frac{1}{2}$ of these amounts.

a)

$\frac{1}{2}$ of 8 is ⬜.

> I will cross one thing out every time I share it.

b)

$\frac{1}{2}$ of 14 is ⬜.

2 Find $\frac{1}{2}$ of these amounts.

a)

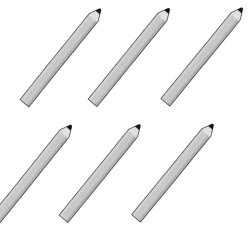

$\frac{1}{2}$ of 6 is ⬜.

b)

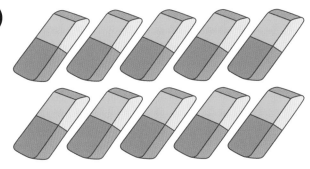

$\frac{⬜}{⬜}$ of 10 is ⬜.

3 Copy each shape.

Shade $\frac{1}{2}$ of the shape.

CHALLENGE

a)

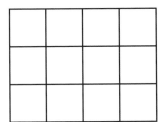

$\frac{⬜}{⬜}$ of ⬜ = ⬜.

b)

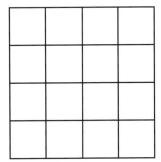

$\frac{⬜}{⬜}$ of ⬜ = ⬜.

171

→ Practice book 2B p122

Recognising a quarter ($\frac{1}{4}$)

Discover

The team must run round the track once. Each runner in the team must run the same distance.

A   B   C   D

1 **a)** Runner A starts.

He runs round half of the track.

Has he run too far?

Explain how you know.

b) How much of the track does each runner have to run to make it equal?

Share

I can draw the path of runner A on the track or put counters where he starts and ends.

a)

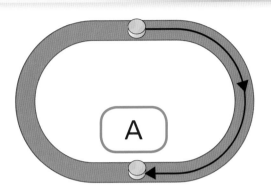

Runner A has gone too far because the other runners must each run less than $\frac{1}{2}$ of the track.

b)

I used counters to show where each runner will start.

I used a ruler and split the running track into four equal parts.

Each runner must run $\frac{1}{4}$ of the running track to make it equal.

I know that a quarter is one of four equal parts.

Think together

1 At lunchtime three children compare their sandwiches.

Which children's sandwiches have been cut into quarters?

How do you know?

Kath's sandwich

Lena's sandwich

Rob's sandwich

_____ sandwiches have been cut into quarters

because _____ .

2 Joey

I have split my table into quarters.

Fred

No, I have split my table into quarters.

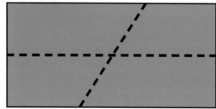 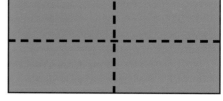

Who is correct?

How do you know?

_____ is correct because _____

174

3 Here is $\frac{1}{4}$ of a shape.

a) Which shape is it from?

A

C

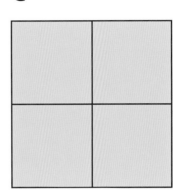

B

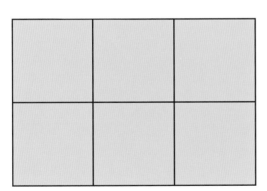

D

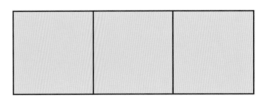

The $\frac{1}{4}$ is from shape ☐.

b) Draw a different shape it could be from.

175

→ **Practice book 2B p125**

Finding a quarter

Discover

Ola   Matt   Em   Josh

1 **a)** Can the counters be split into four equal groups?

b) How many counters will each child get?

Share

a)

I split the counters into equal groups by sharing. I gave the counters out one by one. Each child got the same number of counters.

The counters can be split into four equal groups.

b)

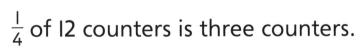

Four equal groups is the same as quarters.

$\frac{1}{4}$ of 12 counters is three counters.

Each child will get three counters.

Think together

①

Share the counters between the children.

How many counters will each child get?

$\frac{1}{4}$ of 20 is ☐.

Each child will get ☐ counters.

② Mr Singh is sharing pencils between four pots.

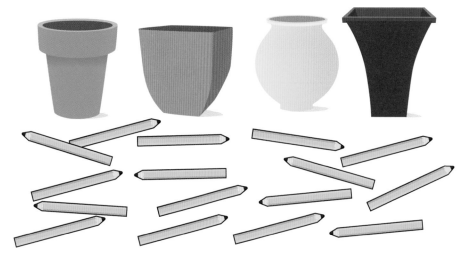

How many pencils will be in each pot?

$\frac{1}{4}$ of 16 is ☐.

There will be ☐ pencils in each pot.

CHALLENGE

3 **a)** Lucy has 13 cubes.

She wants to split them into quarters.

She shares them into four groups.

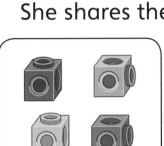  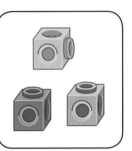 

$\frac{1}{4}$ of 13 = 3

Is Lucy correct? Explain your answer.

b) Harry has 10 cubes.

How many more cubes does he need to be able to split them into quarters?

I wonder if there is more than one answer.

→ **Practice book 2B p128**

Unit fractions

Discover

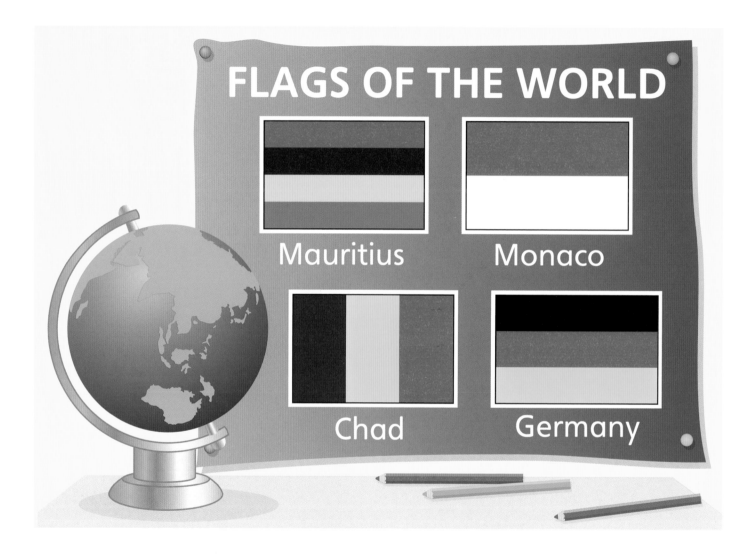

1. a) What fraction of 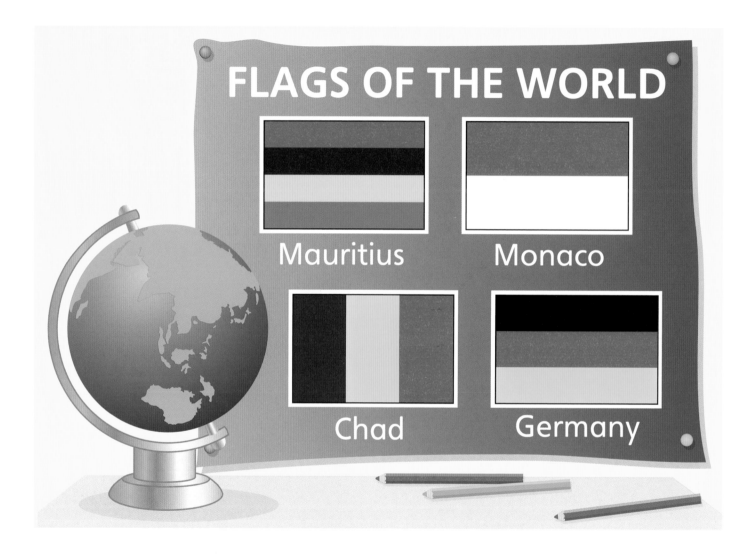 is each stripe?

   What fraction of is each stripe?

   b) What is the same and what is different about the flags?

Share

a)

This flag has 2 equal parts altogether.

Each stripe is 1 part.

Each stripe is $\frac{1}{2}$ of the flag.

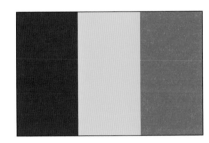

This flag has 3 equal parts altogether.

Each stripe is 1 part.

Each stripe is $\frac{1}{3}$ of the flag.

We call the fraction $\frac{1}{3}$ one **third**.

b) Each flag is split into equal parts.

The number of equal parts is different.

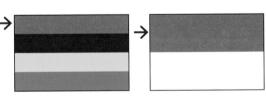 

The flag has	4 parts	2 parts	3 parts	3 parts
Each stripe is	$\frac{1}{4}$	$\frac{1}{2}$	$\frac{1}{3}$	$\frac{1}{3}$

The number of equal parts is the denominator of the fraction.

The numerator of each fraction is 1.

A fraction where the numerator is 1 is called a **unit fraction**.

181

Think together

1 Class 2 have been making their own flags.

Gaby   Tim   Anya   Milo

What fraction of each flag has a star?

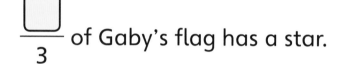

$\dfrac{\Box}{3}$ of Gaby's flag has a star. $\dfrac{1}{\Box}$ of Tim's flag has a star.

$\dfrac{\Box}{\Box}$ of Anya's flag has a star. $\dfrac{\Box}{\Box}$ of Milo's flag has a star.

2 **a)** What fraction of each shape is shaded?

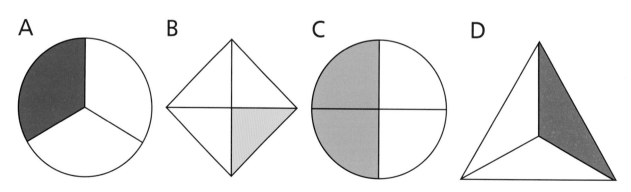

A   B   C   D

b) Which of these are unit fractions?

Explain how you know.

3 Find $\frac{1}{3}$ of each of these.

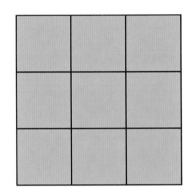

$\frac{1}{3}$ of 6 = ☐

$\frac{1}{3}$ of 9 = ☐

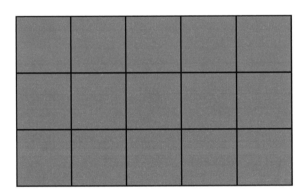

$\frac{1}{3}$ of 15 = ☐

I think I need to divide each into 3 equal parts.

Understanding other fractions

Discover

Lily Noah Ola

1 **a)** What fraction of the children are girls?

b) Ola's kite is $\frac{3}{4}$ red.

Draw the kite.

Share

a)

There are **3** children.

The denominator is **3**.

2 of the children are girls.

The numerator is **2**.

$\frac{2}{3}$ of the children are girls.

This is a **non-unit fraction**. What do you notice about the numerator?

$\frac{2}{3}$ is read as two thirds and $\frac{3}{4}$ is read as three quarters.

b) $\frac{3}{4}$ of the kite is red.

The denominator is **4**.

So there are **4** equal parts.

The numerator is **3**.

So **3** parts are red.

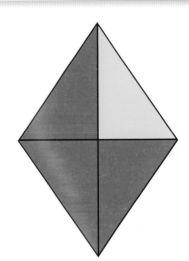

185

Think together

1 Complete the sentences.

This kite is made up of three equal parts.

The denominator is ☐.

Two parts are yellow.

The numerator is ☐.

$\frac{\square}{\square}$ of the kite is yellow.

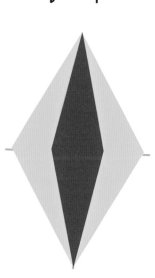

> Equal parts do not always have to look the same.

2

A   B   C   D   E

a) Which kites show $\frac{3}{4}$ shaded?

b) Which kites have a unit fraction shaded?

c) Which kites have non-unit fractions shaded?

3 Is each sentence true or false?

a)

$\frac{2}{3}$ of the fruit are apples.

b)

$\frac{3}{4}$ of the children are boys.

c)

$\frac{2}{4}$ of the animals are cats.

If the denominators are the same, I wonder if non-unit fractions are always greater than unit fractions.

187

$\frac{1}{2}$ and $\frac{2}{4}$

Discover

1: Get a piece of paper

2: Fold it in half

3: Colour it in

4: Fold it in half again

5: Unfold your paper

1 **a)** Let's follow the instructions. What do you notice?

What fraction is shaded?

b) Is it the same with other shapes?

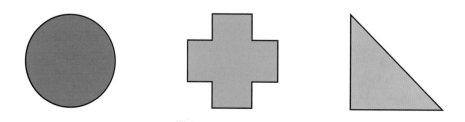

Share

a) Step I

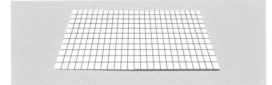

Step 2

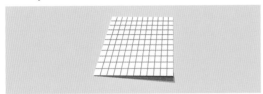

Step 3

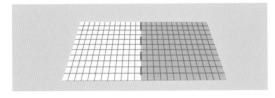

Step 4

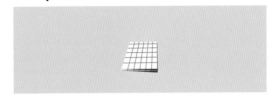

Step 5

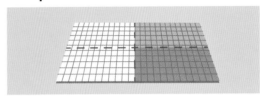

> I checked by cutting the $\frac{1}{2}$ out and placing it on top of $\frac{2}{4}$. They were the same size!

The paper is now divided into quarters.

$\frac{1}{2}$ of the paper is shaded. $\frac{1}{2}$ and $\frac{2}{4}$ are **equivalent**.

b) It is the same with the other shapes.

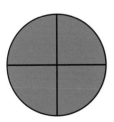 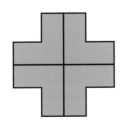 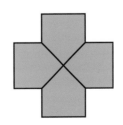 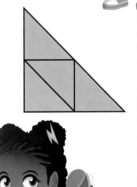

> I can find lots of different ways to show halves and quarters.

Think together

1   Get two strips of paper.

They need to be the same size.

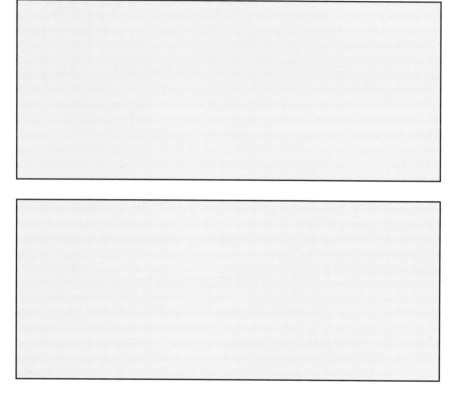

How can you split the strips of paper
to show that $\frac{1}{2}$ and $\frac{2}{4}$ are equal?

I can find
different ways
to show this.

2 **a)** Find $\frac{1}{2}$ of 8.

$\frac{1}{2}$ of 8 is ☐.

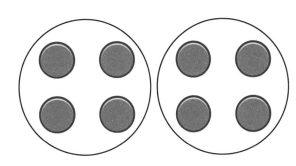

b) Find $\frac{1}{4}$ of 8.

What is $\frac{2}{4}$ of 8?

$\frac{1}{4}$ of 8 is ☐.

$\frac{2}{4}$ of 8 is ☐.

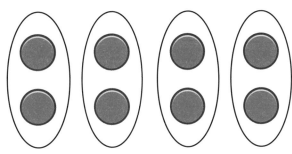

What do you notice about your answers? Why do you think this is the case?

3 Tami says that this bar model can help her solve $\frac{2}{4}$ of 12.

CHALLENGE

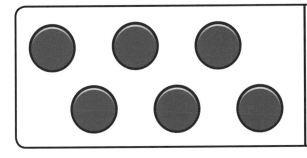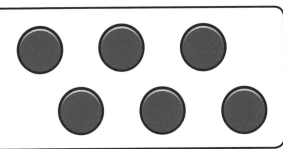

Do you agree?

Explain why.

191

→ Practice book 2B p137

Finding $\frac{3}{4}$

Discover

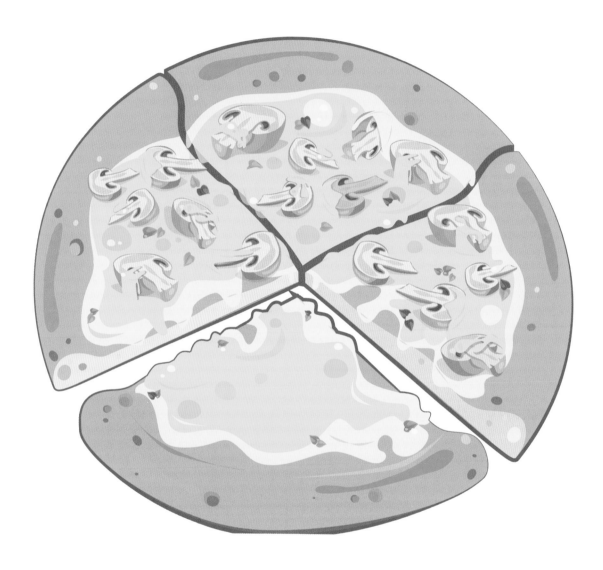

1 **a)** What fraction of the pizza has ?

b) What fraction of the pizza does **not** have any ?

192

Share

a) There are four equal slices of pizza.

Each slice is one quarter of the pizza.

3 out of 4 of the equal parts have .

3 out of 4 equal parts can be written as $\frac{3}{4}$ or three-quarters.

$\frac{3}{4}$ of the pizza has .

> $\frac{3}{4}$ is an example of a non-unit fraction.

b) I out of 4 equal parts does not have any .

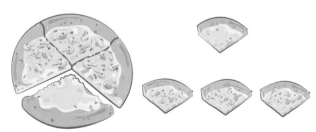

I out of 4 equal parts is written as $\frac{1}{4}$ or one-quarter.

$\frac{1}{4}$ of the pizza does not have any .

Think together

1. Gino has eight  .

   He shares them equally between four people.

   How many does each person get?

   a) How many does he give to one person?

      $\frac{1}{4}$ of 8 = ☐

      He gives ☐ to one person.

   b) How many does he give to three people?

      $\frac{3}{4}$ of 8 = ☐

      He gives ☐ to three people.

2 Which shapes show $\frac{3}{4}$ shaded?

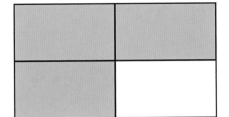
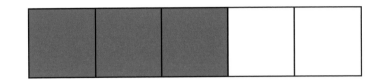

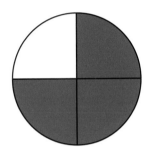
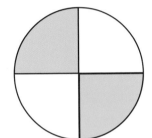
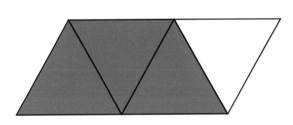

3 What fraction of the shape is shaded?

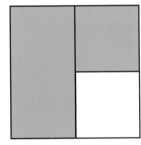

$\dfrac{\square}{\square}$ is shaded.

CHALLENGE

Is the shape split into equal parts? I can see a half and a quarter.

Could we write $\frac{1}{2}$ as another fraction?

195

→ Practice book 2B p140

Understanding a whole

Discover

Jack's sandwich   Maya's sandwich

1 **a)** What fraction is Jack's sandwich cut into?

b) What is different about Maya's sandwich?

What is the same?

Share

a) Jack's sandwich is cut into halves.

He has 2 halves.

2 halves equal one whole.

$\frac{2}{2} = 1$

b) Maya's sandwich is cut into quarters.

She has 4 quarters.

She has one whole sandwich.

4 quarters equal one whole.

$\frac{4}{4} = 1$

The numerator and denominator are the same.

I wonder if the fraction is always one whole when they are the same.

$\frac{4}{4} = 1$ $\frac{2}{2} = 1$ $\frac{3}{3} = 1$

Think together

1 What fraction of each shape is shaded?

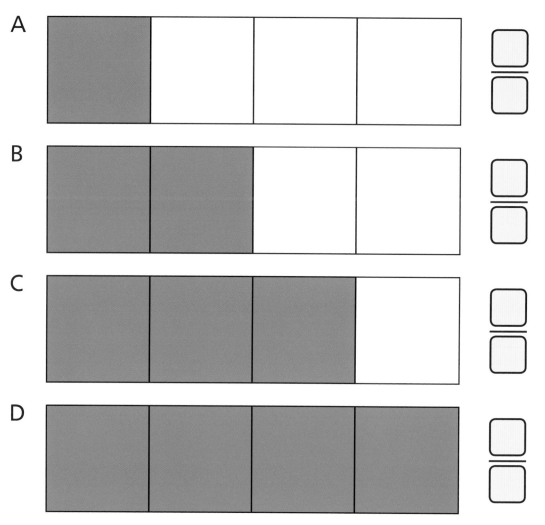

A

B

C

D

Which diagram has the whole shaded? _____

2 Which fractions are equal to one whole?

$\frac{3}{4}$ $\frac{3}{3}$ $\frac{2}{2}$ $\frac{1}{2}$ $\frac{4}{4}$

3 Complete the number sentences.

_____ and _____ equals one whole.

CHALLENGE

a)

$\frac{1}{2} + \frac{\square}{\square} = 1$

I will see if one third and one third equals one whole.

b)

$\frac{\square}{\square} + \frac{\square}{\square} = 1$

c)

$\frac{3}{4} + \frac{\square}{\square} = 1$

→ Practice book 2B p143

Understanding whole and parts

Discover

I　**a)** How many **whole** chocolate bars are there, and how many parts?

　　b) What fraction is needed to make 4 **whole** chocolate bars?

Share

a) There are 3 whole chocolate bars.

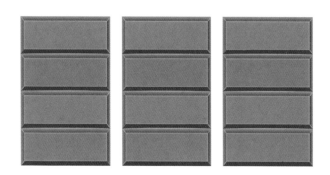

There are also 3 out of 4 parts.

This is $\frac{3}{4}$.

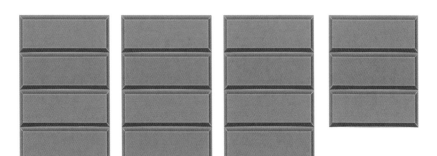

In total, there are 3 and $\frac{3}{4}$ chocolate bars.

We write this as $3\frac{3}{4}$.

b)

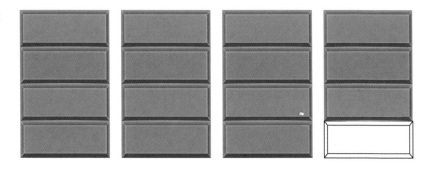

Another $\frac{1}{4}$ is needed to make 4 whole bars.

Think together

 a) How many pizzas altogether?

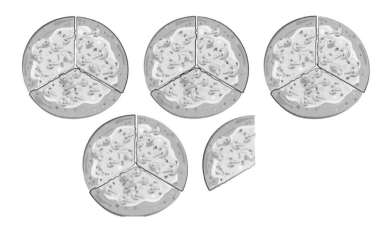

There are _____ and

_____ pizzas.

We can write this as $\boxed{}\dfrac{\boxed{}}{\boxed{}}$.

b) What fraction is needed to make five whole pizzas?

$\dfrac{\boxed{}}{\boxed{}}$ is needed to make five whole pizzas.

2 Complete the table.

	Wholes	Part
$2\frac{1}{2}$	2	
$7\frac{3}{4}$		$\frac{3}{4}$
	5	$\frac{1}{4}$
$9\frac{3}{4}$		

3 Three children share this chocolate equally.

What fraction does each child get?

Each child gets _____ .

I will share each bar.

I will give one bar to each child and share the 4th bar.

203

Counting in halves

Discover

1 **a)** Count in halves to see how many apples there are.

b) How many whole apples are there?

How many extra parts?

Share

a)

$\frac{1}{2}$; 1; 1 and $\frac{1}{2}$; 2; 2 and $\frac{1}{2}$ ...

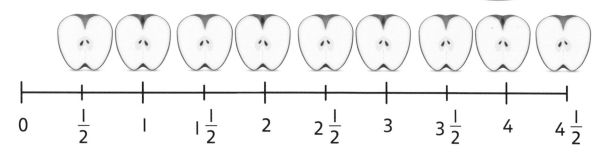

| 0 | $\frac{1}{2}$ | 1 | $1\frac{1}{2}$ | 2 | $2\frac{1}{2}$ | 3 | $3\frac{1}{2}$ | 4 | $4\frac{1}{2}$ |

b) There are four whole apples.

There is also $\frac{1}{2}$ an apple.

There are $4\frac{1}{2}$ apples in total.

Think together

1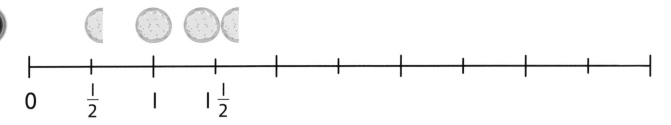

a) What will the next number be?

The next number will be ☐.

b) Count to the end of the number line.

What is the last number?

The last number is ☐.

I remember that $1\frac{1}{2}$ means 1 whole and $\frac{1}{2}$.

2 Draw a number line like this.

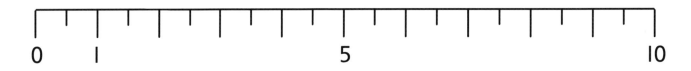

Mark these values on the number line.

$\frac{1}{2}$ 2 $3\frac{1}{2}$ 4   7 $8\frac{1}{2}$

3 **a)** Noah counts up in halves from 0.

Di counts down in halves from 9.

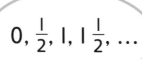

$0, \frac{1}{2}, 1, 1\frac{1}{2}, \dots$

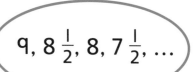

$9, 8\frac{1}{2}, 8, 7\frac{1}{2}, \dots$

Noah

Di

They count at the same time.

What number will they say together?

b) What number would they say together if Di started at 8?

c) What number would they say together if Di started at 7?

I wonder if there is a pattern.

207

→ Practice book 2B p149

Counting in quarters

Discover

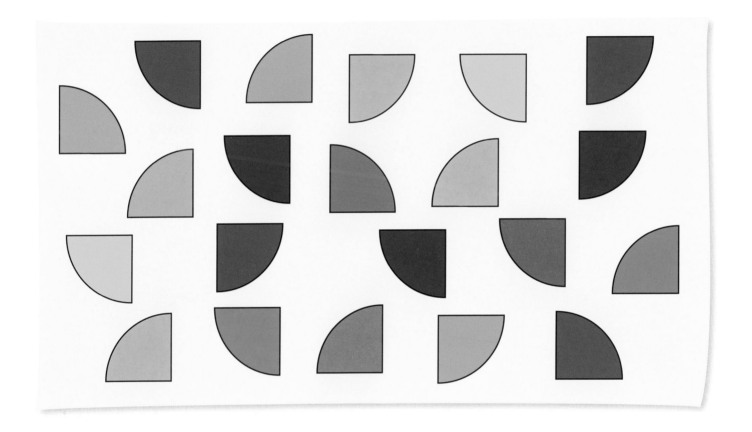

Class 2 made a picture using different coloured quarter circles.

1 **a)** How many circles are there in total?

Give your answer in wholes and quarters.

b) How many more quarters need to be added to make another whole?

Give your answer as a fraction.

Share

a)

I counted each quarter and when I got to $\frac{4}{4}$ I knew it was a whole.

I also used a number line to help me.

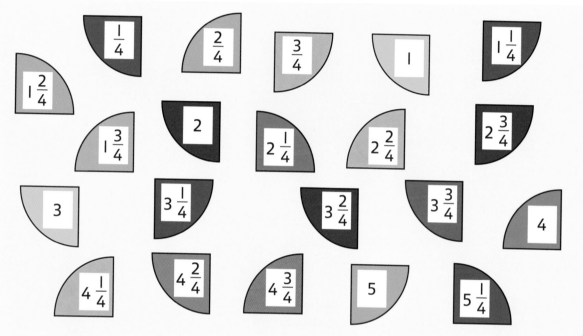

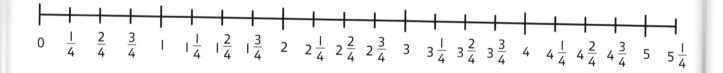

I put the four quarter circles together to make a whole.

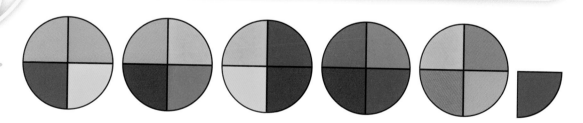

There are 5 whole circles and one quarter in total.

b)

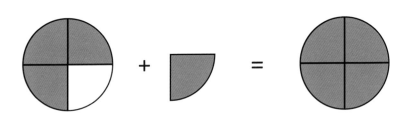

I only need to look at the last part to find how much to make a whole.

We need to add $\frac{3}{4}$ to make a whole (or $\frac{4}{4}$).

Think together

① a) At lunchtime 23 children each ate $\frac{1}{4}$ of a watermelon.

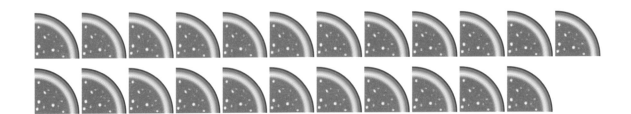

$\boxed{}\dfrac{\boxed{}}{\boxed{}}$ watermelons were eaten in total.

How many watermelons were eaten in total?

b) How many more quarters need to be added to make another whole?

$\boxed{}$ more quarter needs to be added to make another whole.

2 Put the cards in order.

$\boxed{1}$ $\boxed{2\frac{2}{4}}$ $\boxed{\frac{3}{4}}$ $\boxed{2\frac{3}{4}}$

$\boxed{2\frac{1}{4}}$ $\boxed{2}$ $\boxed{0}$ $\boxed{\frac{2}{4}}$ $\boxed{1\frac{2}{4}}$

$\boxed{\frac{1}{4}}$ $\boxed{1\frac{1}{4}}$ $\boxed{1\frac{3}{4}}$ $\boxed{3}$

> I will start with 0.

> I think that I can put the cards in order in more than one way.

3

CHALLENGE

Jack eats $\frac{1}{4}$ of a chocolate bar every day.

How many whole bars will he eat over nine days?

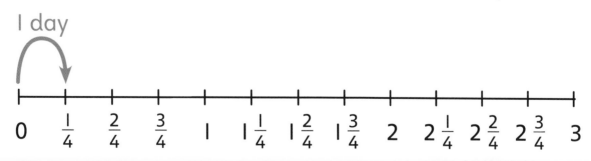

1 day

0   $\frac{1}{4}$ $\frac{2}{4}$ $\frac{3}{4}$ 1 $1\frac{1}{4}$ $1\frac{2}{4}$ $1\frac{3}{4}$ 2 $2\frac{1}{4}$ $2\frac{2}{4}$ $2\frac{3}{4}$ 3

211

→ Practice book 2B p152

End of unit check

Your teacher will ask you these questions.

1 Which shape is $\frac{1}{3}$ shaded?

A
B
C
D

2 What is $\frac{1}{2}$ of 8?

A 16   B 5   C 4   D 3

3 $\dfrac{\square}{\square}$ of 12 = 4

A $\frac{1}{3}$ B $\frac{1}{4}$ C 16   D 8

4 What is the same as $\frac{1}{2}$ of 8?

A $\frac{1}{4}$ of 8   B $\frac{2}{4}$ of 8   C $\frac{1}{3}$ of 8   D $\frac{3}{4}$ of 8

5 Sara cuts a cake into 4 equal pieces.

She eats 3 pieces. How much has she eaten?

A $\frac{1}{4}$ **B** $\frac{2}{4}$ **C** $\frac{3}{4}$ **D** $\frac{4}{4}$

Think!

Here are eight fractions.

$\frac{1}{4}$ $\frac{1}{2}$ $\frac{1}{3}$ $\frac{2}{4}$ $\frac{3}{4}$ $\frac{2}{2}$ $\frac{4}{4}$ $\frac{3}{3}$

Sort the fractions into groups.

Explain how you have sorted them.

These words might help you.

unit fraction

non-unit fraction

quarters

thirds

halves   half

whole   part

→ **Practice book 2B p155**

Wow, we have solved some difficult problems!

Yes, we have! Can we find even better ways to solve problems?

What we have learned

Can you do all these things?

⚡ Divide by 2, 5 and 10

⚡ Identify odd and even numbers

⚡ Make tally charts and pictograms

⚡ Measure and compare length and height

⚡ Recognise properties of 2D and 3D shapes

⚡ Work with fractions

Some of it was difficult, but we did not give up!

Now you are ready for the next books!

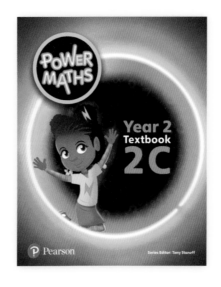

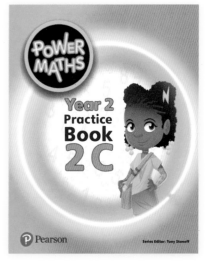